THE
A TO Z
OF
SALES
MANAGEMENT

Original illustrations by Kenneth Aitken

THE
A TO Z
OF
SALES
MANAGEMENT

John Fenton

amacom

A DIVISION OF AMERICAN MANAGEMENT ASSOCIATIONS

Library of Congress Cataloging in Publication Data

Fenton, John, 1938-
   The A to Z of sales management.

   1. Sales management.   I. Title.
HF5438.4.F46 1981   658.8'1   80-69679
ISBN 0-8144-5655-3   AACR1

First published by William Heinemann Ltd., London, England.
Published in the U.S.A. in 1981 by AMACOM,
A division of American Management Associations, New York.

FIRST PRINTING

Acknowledgments

THE WRITING of this book has been something of a combined effort, since one aim has been for it to become the main back-up material to the sales management courses we run at Structured Training Ltd. for the Institute of Sales Management in Great Britain.

Thanks are due to the training team of Structured Training for their contributions to the final work; to Jim Tappenden, sales director of Osro Ltd., for providing so much valuable input for the terms of employment and company-car sections, and to Peter Bosworth, managing director of Sales Control and Record Systems Ltd., for his help on sales force control. And not forgetting my secretary Julie McEwan and my wife Ann, who, respectively, held me back from a too forthright approach to some of the seamier problems of managers today and urged me on to finishing the book almost on time and so avoiding the wrath of my very patient publisher.

Finally, grateful thanks to the companies that were willing to admit that they retained me as a consultant and that have allowed me to use some examples of what I did for them to illustrate this book.

Preface

AT LEAST HALF the sales managers fortunate enough to be reading this are still salesmen at heart; are thinking like salesmen; and are still trying to be accepted as "one of the boys" rather than as leaders of men. They gained their promotion because they were the best salesmen in the company, and able to get on well with the people around them. But because they are still salesmen at heart, they are reluctant to change things they know need changing; to implement effective reporting, planning, and control systems; to introduce more practical ways of motivating and paying the salesmen; and to throw out procedures that have been allowed to continue unaltered since before they themselves joined the company.

They worry constantly about the risk of annoying their salesmen too much and making the situation worse, rather than better. Consequently, they do little but perpetuate the general aura of passive indifference which the company has probably generated for more years than its employees can remember.

This book shows a sales manager how to be different; how to succeed where others have failed; how to get the best out of his salesmen; how to be in complete control of his sales operation; and how to still have his salesmen's respect and friendship.

The book is essentially about people: how to treat, motivate, and lead them to victory against all odds—internal and external.

It is written to separate the forest from the trees and provide guidance on the bare essentials of the task of managing an industrial sales operation—the top priorities of the job.

It shows how to achieve consistent results and how to build a team of salesmen who themselves strive for continual improvement of personal performance. And it shows how the sales manager keeps his cool while all this is happening.

When these priorities have been mastered and fully implemented, the rest will be easy—all the way to the top.

JOHN FENTON

Contents

THE
A TO Z
OF
SALES
MANAGEMENT

The A to Z of Industrial Salesmanship

It's not every author who gets the chance to put in a legitimate plug for another of his books, so early. But in this case, it's *very* legitimate.

You won't ever succeed as a sales manager unless you really know—in depth—what your salesmen should be doing. You don't have to be a better salesman than your salesmen; you *do* need to know in detail how their job must be done and what they have to do to get the required results with a minimum of wasted effort.

The chances are that you have spent quite a few years as a salesman before promotion came your way. Don't fall into the trap of thinking you know all there is to know about selling, based on the strength of your own experience. Think back to the days when *you* were learning how to sell. Who taught you? What kind of training did you get? How much of what you know was picked up off the seat of your pants, out there in the field, or by following the bad habits of other salesmen?

So how do you know that what you've been doing all these years is the *best* way; or the most *economical* way; or the most *effective* way?

Read my first book, *The A to Z of Industrial Salesmanship* (London: William Heinemann Ltd.). Use it to form the basis of the Standards of Performance for your own sales force. Use it in conjunction with this book. Together, the two books will bring you success, just as the methods, techniques, and principles they contain have brought *me* success.

Advertising and Sales Promotion

Don't ever lose sight of the main objective of your advertising and sales promotion activity—to generate inquiries for your sales force o follow up subsequently.

Why advertise at all? Why not leave things completely to the sales force? A recent survey of about 1,000 companies gives the answer.

Size of company	Average number of persons who influence buying decisions	Average number of persons visited by salesmen
Fewer than 200 employees	3.43	1.72
200–400 employees	4.85	1.75
401–1,000 employees	5.81	1.90
More than 1,000 employees	6.50	1.65

So how else do you get to all those decision influencers whom your salesmen are missing? (Plus any potential customers you didn't hitherto know existed, of course.)

DESIGNING ADVERTISEMENTS

Your advertisements and sales promotions should always follow the AIDA format:

ATTENTION	(Picture or simple headline)
INTEREST	(Carrot—preferably about money)
DESIRE	(What *could* be in it for him)
ACTION	(Fill in the coupon or pick up the phone)

Use pictures with life in them, not "still-life" shots of the equipment, grossly overtouched, highlighted and air-brushed.

Never use drawings or sketches of the products. All you are saying to the reader is, "We haven't actually made one yet."

Feature customers or your own people in your advertisements. Those customers will be with you for life. Try to make your picture identify with the reader, or vice versa, so that whatever the people in the picture are doing, the reader will feel like doing, too.

Or try a format which gets the reader *doing* something. The advertisement shown in Figure 1 consistently pulls in over 40 enquiries each time it is used, in a small-circulation British journal which goes to the same people every month. Reasonable proof also that to get consistent results from advertising you need to advertise consistently.

Don't cram too much into too small a space. Blank white space is as powerful in an advertisement as silence is in a selling situation.

Use bookmarks rather than page advertisements in any publication which has a long life as a work of reference. Or use the outside front or back cover or the spine of the book.

One of the best positions to place an advertisement in the average technical or trade journal is on the left-hand page facing the journal's reader enquiry card. Everyone who wants details of anything advertised in that journal will turn to the reader card to send for further information. While they are filling in the card, they must see your advertisement. So they could well circle *your* number as well. Mission accomplished.

WHICH MEDIA TO USE

Don't guess. Get all the readership breakdown details from a selection of journals, and calculate the *true* cost per valid reader.

Say you want to get your advertisement in front of produc-

A checklist for Management

	Tick the Applicable Column	
	Yes	No
1. Do you provide your Salesmen with a standardised method for keeping Customer Records?	☐	☐
2. Do your Salesmen keep their Customer Records up to date — and *USE* them?	☐	☐
3. Do you make sure a Salesman who leaves the company doesn't take his Customer Records with him?	☐	☐
4. Do you know how much Prospecting work your Salesmen need to do to achieve the company's 'New Business' target?	☐	☐
5. If you can answer 'Yes' to question 4, do you know if your Salesmen are actually *doing* the amount of Prospecting work required?	☐	☐
6. Do you receive a detailed plan from your Salesmen of where they will be next week?	☐	☐
7. Are more than 40% of your Salesmen's calls 'By Appointment.'?	☐	☐
8. Do you know how much business your Salesmen are chasing that your company has quoted for?	☐	☐
9. Do you know how much of this business is likely to result in firm orders NEXT MONTH?	☐	☐
10. Do your Salesmen prepare for you a forecast of how much business they reckon they will produce for the company during the next period?	☐	☐
11. Is this forecast in a sufficiently detailed form so that you can pin-point any specific Customer that isn't coming up to expectations?	☐	☐
12. Are the Action Reports you receive from your Salesmen sufficiently legible, detailed and accurate for the company to produce a quotation and be certain it will fulfil the Customer's requirements?	☐	☐
13. Do your Salesmen submit a Weekly Report of the Customers they have called upon — and what happened?	☐	☐
14. If the answer to question 13 is 'Yes', does anyone use the information on the Weekly Reports, rather than just file them away after a general check?	☐	☐
15. Do you know if any Salesmen are neglecting part of your product range?	☐	☐
16. Do you know your company's Average Order Value?	☐	☐
17. Do you know your company's 'Calls to Quotations' ratio?	☐	☐
18. Do you know your company's 'Quotations to Orders' ratio?	☐	☐
Totals	☐	☐

As a manager, all your answers should be YES.

Get a NO more than half a dozen times and you should be starting to worry about exactly how much business your inefficiency is losing the Company.

After that comes the "but what the hell do I do about it with the time I've got available" stage, and that's where we come in.

We have the solution, and it isn't time consuming.

If you would like us to provide a solution to your problems why not contact us?

All enquiries should be made to:

Sales Control & Record Systems Ltd
Concorde House, 24 Warwick New Road, Royal Leamington Spa, CV32 5JH

Figure 1. S.C.R.S. checklist.

tion managers. A certain magazine has a circulation of 20,000, but its readership breakdown indicates that only 10,000 copies go to production managers. Cost of a full-page advertisement is, say, $1,000.

Thus, true cost per valid reader is $\dfrac{\$1,000}{10,000} = 10¢.$

Compare *all* the media you are considering on this basis, unless there are other valid criteria to make you choose differently.

WRITING EDITORIALS

You need to develop the ability to write good editorial copy for trade and technical magazines. A good article is worth umpteen pages of advertisement. Six good articles about six good customers who have benefited significantly from using your products and, when reprinted, you have the contents of a new addition to your range of sales literature—and something much more powerful than your usual brochures.

A good editorial story should be slanted toward the *application* of your products by one or more customers. The article should be 80 percent about the customer and 20 percent about the application and your products. Do it the other way around and no editor will touch the story, nor would it do *you* any good if he or she did.

DON'T FORGET

Always keep your salesmen fully informed about what advertisements and articles are scheduled for publication, and in which media. Give each salesman advance copies and lots of reprints to hand out to customers and prospective customers.

Blue-Tailed-Fly Disease

Do you love working in a panic situation?

Many managers do. Maybe it's a question of adrenaline flow. Everything is left to the last minute. Everyone in the department has to work overtime. The deadline is met, but only after everyone's lost a couple of pounds.

Only the manager who suffers from B.T.F. disease gets any kind of feeling of satisfaction for a job well done, if the job has been done that way. His staff reckon he's a pain, inconsiderate, and irresponsible. And when you get down to brass tacks, it only happens because of a lack of self-discipline, leading to a lack of planning.

Remember the old office joke, hanging on the wall. . . .

If you can keep your head while everyone around you is losing theirs—it means you haven't the slightest idea what's going on.

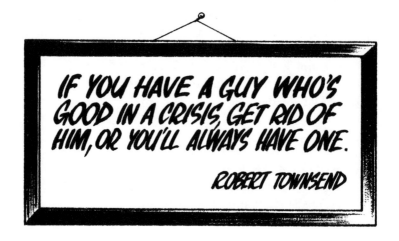

IF YOU HAVE A GUY WHO'S GOOD IN A CRISIS, GET RID OF HIM, OR YOU'LL ALWAYS HAVE ONE.

ROBERT TOWNSEND

. . . Well, the good manager works to be the opposite of this. He keeps his head *and* knows the score. He sets an example and calms everyone down.

He has learned the secret of planning. Start at the point when the job has to be completed, and work *back* toward now; *not* the other way around. From the time plan, establish what has to be done, who has to do it, and delegate each task clearly, building in deadlines for each delegated action. Then relax and let it all happen, being available to mop up any hang-ups or unforeseen problems.

USING YOUR TIME MORE PROFITABLY

A number of business surveys have indicated that the average sales manager works 50 to 60 hours a week. He takes work home with him and lives with a wife who struggles, often unsuccessfully, to keep him human.

He carries his work, often unfinished, back to the office. There he will have one hour alone each day, being interrupted every eight minutes by subordinates or other executives seeking advice or answers to problems. Most of these problems are things other employees are being paid to resolve.

He spends 80 percent of his time communicating and only 20 percent doing creative work.

The Heart Association says this can be fatal.

So set yourself some objectives:

1. To reduce interruptions by 50 percent.
2. To reduce time spent on the telephone by 50 percent.
3. To reduce time spent on correspondence by 30 percent.
4. To double the time spent on planning and thinking.
5. To allow half an hour every day for self-analysis and creativity.

6. To delegate properly an additional 20 percent of your own workload.

7. To make full use of your secretary.

If you need to start by analyzing what you do at present, get your secretary to list everything that happens for a full week. It will frighten you to death.

COSTINGS

If your working year contains 238 days, your salary is $40,000 per year, and the company's overheads are 200 percent, your time is costing this much:

1 minute	$ 1.20
5 minutes	$ 6.00
10 minutes	$ 12.50
30 minutes	$ 36.00
1 hour	$ 72.00
1 day	$504.00

This doesn't include your car and expenses.

Company Cars

Many American industrial companies provide their salesmen and sales managers with a car, and pay all reasonable, properly incurred business expenses for running the car. Some, on the other hand, require their sales staff to provide their own car, and pay a depreciation and running allowance, plus gas and oil costs incurred on business. (I'll deal with this latter method at the end of this section.)

The sales manager cannot ever afford to allow any salesman to abuse in any way the privileges attaching to the company car. Stick to the established rules at all times. If one person gets an edge—like being allowed to tow a trailer, or to take the car on vacation, or to install a quadraphonic stereo system with built-in speakers—the rest of the sales force will expect similar treatment. The sales manager who allows these things will therefore need to budget for the cost over the entire sales force car fleet, or to consider any reduction in residual value which might apply when the cars are traded in for new ones.

CAR USER'S HANDBOOK

The company should provide every user of a company car with an explicit set of instructions covering the car's use. Here's a sample set:

1. Driving Licenses and Authority to Drive Company Cars

(*a*) That the person be in possession of a current driving license and have the company's authority to drive one of its vehicles, which authority must be given by the company's Vice-President, Finance & Administration (VP, F&A).

(*b*) That the person's driving license has been produced for scrutiny by the VP, F&A.

If at any time the person is disqualified from driving, the VP, F&A must be informed immediately.

It is the responsibility of the driver of the vehicle to see that it is not driven by anyone other than authorized company employees. Special written permission must be obtained from the VP, F&A for the car to be used by any other driver not falling into this category.

2. Acceptance of Vehicle and Company Rules

At the time of taking over a company car, the VP, F&A will ask the driver to inspect the vehicle, accept its condition, and sign a form of receipt which will incorporate any existing faults. Additionally all drivers will be asked to sign for a copy of the company's rules for the use of company cars, and their signature will be taken as their acceptance of these rules.

If permission is given for a person other than the authorized driver to use the car, in addition to inspecting the person's driving licence, the VP, F&A must have a signature from that person acknowledging receipt of the company's rules for the use of company cars.

3. Fixtures, Fittings, and Modifications

No fixtures, such as aerials, roof racks, towing apparatus, and stickers, may be attached to company vehicles without prior written permission from the VP, F&A. When vehicles are given back to the company, such attachments must remain unless adequate rectification work is carried out professionally to restore the vehicle to its former condition.

No changes or alterations may be made in the mechanical or structural specification as delivered of any company vehicle.

4. Warranty

When a new car is handed to a driver, a copy of the manufacturer's warranty is also given to the driver. It is the driver's responsibility to ensure that any costs which may arise and which fall under the terms of the warranty are reported to the VP, F&A, *in advance* of any work being carried out. If the driver cannot obtain free repairs from a garage licensed by the manufacturer, no charges may be incurred without prior written permission from the VP, F&A. If any charges are incurred without following this rule, they must be borne by the driver, since the manufacturer will not accept responsibility for work already carried out.

5. *Cleaning and Maintenance*

When a company car has been allocated to a particular driver, it is that person's responsibility to keep the car clean and to ensure that the vehicle is regularly serviced in accordance with the requirements laid down by the manufacturers and specified in the maintenance book of the particular model of car.

Unless contrary arrangements exist in writing between the company and the driver, the company will reimburse the driver for amounts spent on regular servicing, provided that a receipt is submitted to the company, accompanied by a claim for reimbursement detailed on a company expense voucher.

Any other maintenance or repair work or replacement of parts, including tires, must be approved in advance by the company, and reimbursement will only be made against production of an authorization. Full details of the work required and the cost involved must be given.

6. *Fuel and Miscellaneous Problems*

In addition to keeping the vehicle regularly serviced, it is the driver's responsibility to see that the oil level, water level, battery charge, brake fluid, clutch fluid, and tire pressures are kept constantly in the correct state. Gasoline octane ratings, oil grades, and all other fluids used must conform to the manufacturer's recommendations as laid down in the driver's handbook.

Unless contrary arrangements exist in writing between the company and the driver, the company will reimburse the driver only for gas and oil used on company business. Claims must be submitted on an expense voucher signed by the individual and accompanied by receipted bills. All bills should be listed and a deduction shown for that part of the fuel attributable to private mileage.

7. Garaging

No car, whether belonging to the company or privately owned, may be parked on the company's premises without prior consent. Any costs incurred by drivers for garaging cars must be the driver's responsibility.

8. Fines

The company cannot, under any circumstances, accept responsibility for parking or other fines incurred by drivers.

9. Insurance

General. General motor vehicle insurance is expensive and annually getting more so. All vehicles used within the company are insured on a fleet basis, which enables the company to enjoy a larger no-claim bonus than would be possible by insuring individual vehicles. This means, however, that the accident record is calculated on a fleet aggregate, and it is therefore incumbent on every driver to exercise special care with respect to the vehicle under his control; otherwise, he will incur expenses which affect the premium rates for all the cars used by the company. It must be pointed out that in the

United States, every state has jurisdiction over insurance regulations, so the following are only guidelines.

Damage or injury. Although physical damage to company cars is usually not insured, injury to individuals is covered. The driver of any vehicle involved in an accident which causes damage or injury to any person, vehicle, or animal is required to give his name and address, his license number, the name and address of the owner, the registration number of the vehicle, and the name of his insurance company to any person having reasonable grounds for requiring such information.

Claims. It is a condition of the insurance policy that the insurers are notified of *all* third-party accidents even if they are apparently of no consequence. As soon as possible after the accident, the driver must therefore get an accident report form which must be completed and forwarded to the appropriate party. All the information required on the form must be completed, and usually includes the following:

(*a*) The name, addresses, and license number of the third-party driver and the name and address of his insurers.

(*b*) The names and addresses of all passengers in both the company car and the third party's vehicle.

(*c*) Names and addresses of all witnesses. It will be of considerable assistance if statements can be obtained from all witnesses at the time of the accident. Experience shows that if these are not obtained at that time, their value is usually negligible after any subsequent interval.

(*d*) Particulars of the attending officer(s) (name, badge number, precinct, etc.).

A detailed sketch must be provided showing the relative position of the vehicle before and after the accident, together with details of the roads in the vicinity (for example, whether they are major or minor roads, and as many relevant measurements as possible).

If the vehicle belonging to the company cannot be driven, the driver is responsible for making adequate arrangements for the vehicle to be towed to a garage, and the name and address of the garage where the vehicle can be inspected must be stated on the claim form.

An estimate of the required repairs, showing details and cost of both labor and materials, must be obtained.

The driver must not UNDER ANY CIRCUMSTANCES express any opinion one way or another on the degree of responsibility for the accident. Just exchange the particulars mentioned above under *Damage or injury*—and nothing more! This is especially important in cases involving death or injury and leading to an inquest or hearing, since the driver will have to be legally represented and would not wish to prejudice his position in any way.

10. Seat Belts

Seat belts are fitted to all company cars. Drivers and front-seat passengers should wear them on *all* journeys.

11. Automobile Registration

The registration for each vehicle will automatically be renewed when due, but in the event that the new registration is not received by the driver within 14 days of the expiration date, the appropriate company official should be immediately notified by telephone.

12. General Security

At all times when leaving the vehicle unattended, the driver must ensure that all windows are closed, the ignition key removed, and the vehicle securely locked.

13. Personal Baggage

Articles of any kind carried in the vehicle and not the property of the company are at the risk of the owner of the property, and the company accepts no responsibility whatsoever for such property.

14. Permitted Use

Subject to the restrictions already stipulated, private vehicles may only be used for social, domestic, and pleasure purposes and for the business of the company, excluding the carriage of passengers for hire. Company vehicles may not be used for any type of sport, including racing or rallying, whether on the public highway or on private land. Commercial vehicles may only be used in connection with the company's business.

15. Priority Use

The company reserves the right to take back any car at any time should an occasion arise where the company has an imperative need for the vehicle.

CAR SIZE AND STATUS

"Never fall in love with the company car" is the suggestion I make in my first book, yet many salesmen and sales executives still fall into this emotional trap and wind up in trouble.

More people see status in a larger car than in any other single item they own or have the use of. Many companies reward consistent performance by giving that person a slightly better car than his colleagues, but this only acts as a motivating factor if the companies are also prepared to give the person back his smaller car if he *stops* performing.

If a sales manager has any say in the matter, he shouldn't

allow the size of the car given to the company accountant or the plant manager to have any influence on the most *suitable* car for the sales force. The average annual mileage for an industrial salesman in 1976 was 28,000 miles. The average for sales managers was 32,000 miles. Comfort, safety, and freedom from fatigue are key factors in a salesman's consistent performance.

CREDIT CARDS

A good way to minimize business delays because of car breakdowns is for the company to allocate its sales force credit cards. These enable the salesman to rent a car at a local office without delays, the charges being billed directly to the company.

THE SALESMAN'S OWN CAR

Most people look after things that belong to them better than they look after other people's property. They also normally get greater satisfaction from driving a car they have chosen themselves. There are no restrictions on the use of the car to annoy its owner or his wife.

Most American firms encourage their salesmen to buy their own cars. Most companies operating this way help by offering interest-free loans, but condition these loans by specifying size limits for the car and maximum life before it should be renewed. The owner then receives a depreciation and maintenance allowance and is reimbursed for business gasoline and oil or receives an additional mileage allowance to cover gas and oil. Don't ask for guideline allowance figures; they change almost every month.

HOW TO SPOT A COMPANY CAR

1. They travel faster in ALL gears, especially reverse.

2. They accelerate at a phenomenal rate.

3. They enjoy a much shorter braking distance.

4. They have a much tighter turning circle.

5. They can take ramps at twice the speed of private cars.

6. Battery, water, oil and tire pressures are not needed to be checked nearly so often.

7. The floor is shaped just like an ashtray.

8. They burn only unleaded high-test or premium gasoline.

9. They do not require to be garaged at night.

10. Can be driven for up to 100 miles with the oil warning light flashing.

11. They need cleaning less often.

12. The suspension is reinforced to allow carriage of concrete slabs and other heavy building materials.

13. They are adapted to allow reverse gear to be engaged while the car is still moving forwards.

14. The tire walls are designed to allow bumping into and over curbs.

15. Unusual and alarming engine noises are easily eliminated by the adjustment of the fitted radio volume control.

16. No security needed. May be left anywhere, unlocked, with the keys in the ignition.

Con Artists and Malingerers

If you develop a gut feeling that one of your salesmen is not playing fair, then take positive action fast; otherwise, the feeling will grow into a cancerous attitude against the man which will insidiously mar your working relationship.

Find out for sure whether he takes his kids to school each morning, collects them each afternoon, fails to make all the calls his reports say he has, plays golf on alternate Wednesdays and Fridays, or whatever.

And if he does, invite him into your office and present him with the facts. Then tell him he's being a fool, ask him to choose between resigning and doing the job properly, and if he decides to carry on, confirm the discussion with a confidential memo.

Check again seven weeks later. If he's still conning the company or attending interviews for another job, fire him on the spot. No notice, no salary *in lieu*. Then call the rest of the team together and tell them all precisely what you have done and why. After that, no one's in any doubt about what will happen to con artists and malingerers in the organization.

Of course, it follows that school trips, weekday golf, and so on, are all out for you.

Credit Control

Don't ever let the accounts department chase your customers for payments without first checking with you or with a senior official in your sales office to make sure there are no good reasons for the delay in payment. That way you'll avoid what could be a great embarrassment.

Personally, I believe it is up to the salesman to secure payment of overdue accounts. After all, he took the order, and he should have checked out the customer for creditworthiness and established the ground rules for payment at the order-acceptance stage.

Okay, I know life isn't always like that. But try to get as near the optimum as you can.

If your company is blessed with its own computer, there is one little gimmick you might find useful as well as effective in securing payment without further ado.

Get the *computer* to write the customer a letter—as a print-out. Like this:

I am the Bloggs Pumps Computer.

As yet, no one but me knows that there is a balance out-standing on your July account.

If, however, I have not processed a payment from you within 14 days, I am programmed to tell the office man-ager, who will then deal with the matter. Why should we involve him?

Curbside Conferences

Why do most sales managers avoid regularly spending a day with each of their salesmen, making just ordinary calls? It isn't just because they are always too busy; I think it is because a clear-cut objective for the day's visit has never been estab-lished and so there is a feeling of embarrassment between manager and salesman and often a feeling on the part of the salesman that his manager is only checking up on him.

Which he is—but there is a right way and a wrong way to check up.

Here's a way for you to make these days with the salesmen as

Selling Skills	Above Standard	Standard	Needs Improvement
1. PLANNING PREPARATION			
a) Information	Has all the relevant information for every call.	Has most of the relevant information for every call.	Has some relevant information for most calls.
b) Sales tools	Always carries all relevant equipment, stationery, etc.	Invariably carries some relevant equipment, stationery, etc.	Often carries some relevant equipment, stationery, etc.
c) Action plan	Always prepares detailed action plan.	Invariably prepares action plan.	Often prepares an action plan.
2. APPROACH			
a) Opening remarks	Always gains attention by using skillful opening phrases and "carrots" (lead-ins).	Occasionally fails to gain attention because of failure to use "carrots."	Seldom uses "carrots" or skillful opening phrases.
b) Sales aids	Always uses a sales aid where appropriate.	Often uses a sales aid in approach.	Seldom uses a sales aid in approach.
3. PRESENTATION			
a) Product knowledge	Fully conversant with all products and applications.	Well-informed about all products and applications.	Has some knowledge of most products and applications.
b) Selling points	Knows and uses all selling points for all products.	Knows most selling points for all products.	Knows some selling points for most products.
c) Buyer benefits	Always translates selling points into benefits.	Occasionally fails to translate selling points into benefits.	Sometimes translates selling points into benefits.
d) Buying motives	Always makes presentation appeal to buyer's motives.	Occasionally fails to make presentation appeal to buyer's motives.	Often fails to make presentation appeal to buyer's motives.

Figure 2. Personal skills standards.

Selling Skills	Above Standard	Standard	Needs Improvement
e) Sales aids	Always uses them to maximum advantage.	Always uses them, often to maximum advantage.	Sometimes uses sales aids, to advantage.
f) Handling objections	Always handles objections successfully, leaving the buyer satisfied.	Handles most objections successfully, leaving the buyer satisfied.	Handles some objections successfully, does not always leave the buyer satisfied.
g) Selling sequence	Always uses correct sequence.	Often uses correct sequence.	Seldom uses correct sequence.
h) Rental	Always tries to sell rental.	Often tries to sell rental.	Seldom tries to sell rental.

4. CLOSING THE SALE

Selling Skills	Above Standard	Standard	Needs Improvement
a) Buying signals	Always recognizes and acts upon buying signals.	Occasionally fails to recognize and act upon buying signals.	Often fails to recognize and act upon buying signals.
b) Method of close	Always uses the most appropriate style of close.	Occasionally fails to use the appropriate style of close.	Often fails to use the appropriate style of close.
c) Departure drill	Always thanks, reassures, or questions buyer as appropriate.	Occasionally fails to thank, reassure, or question the buyer as appropriate.	Often fails to thank, reassure, or question the buyer as appropriate.

5. CALL ANALYSIS

Selling Skills	Above Standard	Standard	Needs Improvement
a) Records/reports and correspondence	Always completed accurately, promptly, and up to date.	Occasionally fails to complete accurately, promptly, and up to date.	Always completed but not always accurate, prompt, and up to date.
b) Information	Always records information for future use.	Occasionally fails to record information for future use.	Sometimes records information for future use.
c) Self-analysis	Invariably analyzes personal performance.	Often analyzes personal performance.	Seldom analyzes personal performance.

Administration Skills	Above Standard	Standard	Needs Improvement
6. TERRITORY MANAGEMENT			
a) Use of selling time	Plans very carefully and wastes no time.	Plans carefully, and wastes little time.	Does not plan, and wastes time on unnecessary journeys.
b) Competitors' activities	Actively seeks relevant information and keeps everybody informed.	Generally good at reporting information.	Seldom reports competitor activity.
c) Territory development	Constantly active and opening new a/cs in addition to developing existing a/cs.	Developing existing a/cs and occasionally opening new a/cs.	Inclined to concentrate on existing business, seldom trying to gain new customers.
7. PERSONAL			
a) Appearance	Always exceptionally well-groomed and a credit to his company.	Always well-groomed and a credit to his company.	Not always well-groomed and a credit to his company.
b) Attitude	Always expresses a positive attitude toward the company and its products, policies, and customers.	Occasionally fails to express a positive attitude toward the company and its products, policies, and customers.	Often expresses a negative attitude toward the company and its products, policies, and customers.

8. OTHER RELEVANT POINTS

ON-GOING PERSONAL SKILLS RECORD

By using the Performance Standards as a guide, rate performance under the following headings:

A = Above Standard B = Standard C = Needs Improvement

Date of appraisal												
1 PLANNING PREPARATION												
a) Information												
b) Sales tools												
c) Action plan												
2 APPROACH												
a) Opening remarks												
b) Sales aids												
3 PRESENTATION												
a) Product Knowledge												
b) Selling points												
c) Buyer benefits												
d) Buying motives												
e) Sales aids												
f) Handling objections												
g) Selling sequence												
h) Rental												
4 CLOSING THE SALE												
a) Buying signals												
b) Method of Close												
c) Departure drill												
5 CALL ANALYSIS												
a) Records/reports/correspondence												
b) Information												
c) Self analysis												
6 TERRITORY MANAGEMENT												
a) Use of Selling time												
b) Competitors' activities												
c) Territory Development												
7 PERSONAL												
a) Appearance												
b) Attitude												
Appraisor's Signature												

At the end of each appraisal day, the Sales Manager should complete this form, with the salesman, discussing the various areas where improvement is necessary in relation to the day's work. The Sales Manager should give recommendations and guidance on how the agreed weaknesses should be improved. No allowances should be made for inexperience.

Figure 3.   Ongoing personal skills record.

effective as possible and banish all that bad feeling. The illustrations shown in Figures 2 and 3 are of a document used by firms like Ross Foods and G.K.N. Sankey Automatic Vending Division to keep their salesmen and their sales managers really on their toes. The document, called *Personal Selling Standards and Performance Record*, forms the basis for a one-day-per-month field visit, with both salesman and manager clearly understanding what is expected. On each field visit, the manager assesses the salesman on 24 different aspects of his job. At the end of the day, they both get together for a Curbside Conference on the day's activities, and *agree* on the assessments.

Then salesman and manager agree together on what action the salesman needs to take in the ensuing month, to improve any aspects that are below par. One month later, they can see what improvement has occurred—and so on. Their main aim—to have all 24 aspects consistently above standard.

Some words of warning: During the day's calls, you must sit back and let the salesman do all the work; don't let him introduced you as his boss, only as "Mr. ____ from headquarters, out with me today as part of a familiarization exercise." And when you start the Curbside Conference, no recriminations. It's not a hatchet meeting.

Customer Records

Always provide your salesmen with a standard system of customer records, one that is easy to use and easy to keep up to date.

If your salesmen spend the majority of their time selling on a repeat-business basis, provide them with customer record files—not cards—foolscap size. Then all the assorted paper-

Figure 4.   Customer record file.

work they need to keep on each customer can be stored in one place, in the customer record file, and the sides of the file itself become the call record. Figure 4 shows a typical customer record file.

A good filing system for customer record cards or files works on a date-of-next-call basis, not alphabetically. Thus, after a call, the salesman fills in the details on his card or file, plus the date and objective of the *next* call, which he has set with the customer before departing. The record is filed back into the

salesman's system in the month during which the next call is
due. So, at the end of, say, May, every customer due for a call
during June is already filed under June. No time-consuming
sorting through the records every week to establish who's due
for a call. Result—happier salesmen.

If a salesman leaves, make sure you get all his records back.
Everything is legally company property anyway, even any
cards or books he may have purchased himself. All these records, if properly maintained, are essential to the salesman who
replaces the man leaving. They can reduce his initial time up
to full effectiveness by six months—and you know how much
money that will save, and how much extra business it will
produce.

Decision Making

Most managers are lousy decision makers.

Maybe it's that feeling of insecurity generated by the chairman. Or maybe it's just that making a decision on something
when you've run out of time before all the facts have been
collected gives you a feeling that being wrong is going to come
back to haunt you, while everyone else is going to escape
scot-free.

There used to be a simple rule on decision making in the
businessman's rule book: "Any decision is better than none at
all." This rule is still true today. Decisions made that are subsequently found to be wrong can be changed, and changed
fast.

But there are a few more rules that can reduce the chances
of being wrong:

DECISIONS ABOUT SOLVING PROBLEMS

1. Define the problem. A problem correctly defined is a problem 80 percent solved.
2. Pinpoint the causes of the problem. You cannot find a solution until you are sure about the causes.
3. Establish the possible solutions.
4. Decide on the best solution, selected from all possible solutions.
5. Implement the best solution—fast and firmly.

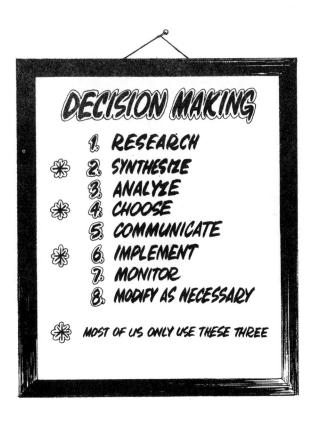

DECISIONS ON PEOPLE PROBLEMS

1. Get all the facts. Get both sides of the story. Talk to everyone involved. Check back on the records. Gauge opinions, attitudes, and feelings.
2. Don't jump to conclusions. Don't allow your own personal feelings to interfere. Fit all the facts together and make sure the complete jigsaw puzzle makes sense.
3. Consider all possible actions. Check company policies. Consult other executives if you feel this is necessary. Consider the effort of your action on the individual, your team, and the rest of the company. Don't panic and chicken out if you still think you're right.
4. Take action. And don't ever pass the buck to someone else.
5. Check the results of the action. Did you achieve your objective?

Exhibitions

If you get stuck with the task of organizing your company's booth at a trade exhibition, you'll find it one of the most time-consuming and nerve-racking jobs you've ever had. There are about 60 separate events that go into the planning of a trade booth, from conception or decision to exhibit, to opening day.

Done properly, the organizing takes a year. Yet most companies only start getting down to it about three months before the exhibition itself.

Planning an exhibition booth entails using a process called Project Management. It is different and separate from the day-to-day disciplines in the company.

A "project" like an exhibition booth has deadline urgency. It has a beginning, a middle, and an end. The end is the date by which the project has to be completed.

A project is superimposed on other work, and is handled by people who have their regular responsibilities to discharge as well.

A project runs across departmental boundaries and needs to harness people with a variety of skills, scattered through different departments.

A project is a pioneering enterprise. There is much greater probability of unforeseen problems.

The top ten rules of Project Management are as follows:

THE TOP TEN RULES OF PROJECT MANAGEMENT

1. *Agree on objectives.* The objectives must be established at the first meeting, and agreed to by everyone present.

2. *Establish command.* The man in charge must be accepted as carrying the full authority necessary to bring the project to a successful conclusion.

3. *Establish responsibilities.* The separate responsibilities for sections or stages of the project must be clearly defined and each one firmly allocated to a single manager.

4. *Plan all dates backward from D-Day.* A detailed project planning chart must be drawn up, with the dates worked out to give sufficient time to avoid last-minute panic. The chart and dates must be circulated to all those responsible.

5. *Every manager must have his own calendar.* As well as the overall project chart, each responsible manager must have his own calendar of key dates.

6. *Arrange key meetings a long way in advance.* There will not be many key meetings which all the project team managers have to attend, but they are likely to be almost impossible to

arrange at short notice. It is no bad thing to set them all at the first meeting, together with agreement on what actions must be completed and what information obtained in time for each.

7. *Circulate information religiously.* This includes, in particular, minutes of all meetings—details of each person's responsibilities; details of all action decisions; information on any changes in the project program; and the complete project chart as soon as it is complete and whenever it is revised.

8. *Chase progress relentlessly.* Especially when the project is superimposed on other work, constant reminders are essential. The project leader's secretary will probably need a separate desk diary to enter the successive targeted completion dates.

9. *Check budgets regularly.* The project leader must get each manager to let him have a detailed breakdown of his budget as soon as possible, and must regularly compare committed expenditure with the budget figure, issuing red alerts the moment he sees a hint of overspending.

10. *Resist alterations ruthlessly.* A few alterations may be inevitable, and some more may be too important to exclude; but remember that it is alterations after the program is agreed on that constitute the greatest single hazard to the enterprise. So it is worth taking a lot of trouble to ensure that everyone who might contribute or be affected has been consulted and has had a chance to have his say before you lock off the program.

D-DAY

When the day of the exhibition finally arrives, there are at least three critical things to have considered:

1. That you have a booth manager who has been delegated complete authority, even over the chairman.
2. That you have a booth-manning rotation that provides

for a maximum of two-hour-long shifts. (That's all the
guards outside the White House do!)
3. That you have a proper system for logging enquiries.

Figure 5 shows an exhibition enquiry form that I designed for a
stand at the 1976 Machine Tool Exhibition. The pad of forms
went inside a survey pad and, just in case a booth salesman was
surprised by a prospective customer at a time he was not carrying his survey pad (sacrilege indeed!), we also produced a
miniature version for his jacket pocket. This particular
exhibitor logged more than 1,200 enquiries during the 1976
show, using this system.

Expense Accounts

If you operate a lunch or subsistence allowance, make sure
you keep up with the current costs of lunches, hotel accommodations, dinners, etc. If your allowances are out of phase
with the going rates, you'll demotivate your salesmen and encourage them to fudge their expense claims.

It is a measure of the attitudes that exist within some sales
forces that even when the company states clearly that a lunch
allowance is intended to cover only the *difference* between a
lunch taken outside and one taken in the factory cafeteria (for
which all workers have to pay), this still seems to be a constant
cause of demotivation and complaints that the allowance is too
low.

Make sure the expenses claim form used by your salesman is
designed to give you the kind of detailed information for which
you need to look. Also get the claim form to separate out sales
tax. You'll be your company accountant's friend for life.

Figure 6 shows an example of a well-designed monthly expenses claim form.

SMT-PULLMAX
MACH'76 Enquiry

Products of interest

Notes on specific details	Metal Cutting	Metal Forming
General Information	☐ ST 10-220	☐ P31-CNC220
Budget Price	☐ ST 14-220	☐ Pullmax Universal
Quotation	☐ ST20-220	☐ Pullmax Beveller X91
Time Studies	☐ VHF/3/3U/3UBS	☐ Pullmax Ring Roller 731
Demonstration	☐ Unidrill 1000	☐ Kumla Rolls PV7H
		☐ Ursviken Press Brakes
		☐ Ursviken Guillotine
		☐ Wikstroms BW300
		☐ Wikstroms BW225/4DV

Literature taken at MACH'76 stand

☐ General Catalogue m/c   ☐ General Catalogue m/f

Reason for interest

☐ Expanding production   OTHERS

☐ Replacing existing plant

☐ Seeking to reduce labor force

Name _____ Position _____

Company _____

Address _____

_____

Telephone Number _____ Extension _____

Best Time For Sales Engineer To Call _____

Figure 5.   Exhibition enquiry form.

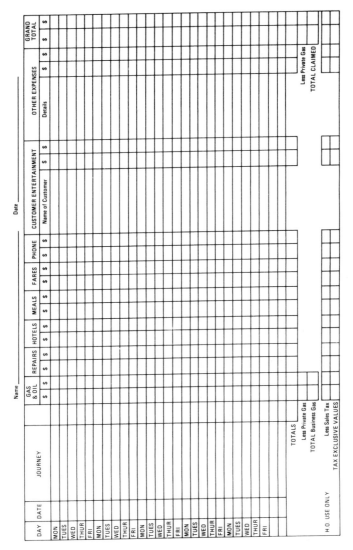

Figure 6.   Monthly expenses claim form.

Forecasting

Your company's sales forecast for next year (or whatever the next selling period may be) has to be put together mainly by your sales force, because it is the sales force that has to be committed to the task of *achieving* the forecast sales.

You'll never really commit a salesman to achieving any objective if he hasn't been involved in deciding what the objective should be, and why.

It takes three months for any salesman to produce a meaningful forecast of the business his territory should produce next year. Not three months' solid work, of course; three months during which the salesman is making his normal calls, but at the same time, asking an additional question or two of everyone he meets, such as, "I've got to produce a forecast of what business will come from my territory next year. Could you give me any idea of what your requirements are likely to be between January and December?" . . . and so on. Think of the commitment they get from the customers for next year, on this basis.

Don't expect an accurate forecast if you give your salesmen a week in which to prepare it. All you'll get is an overall guess based on last year. Totally useless.

Use a form for sales forecasting like the one shown in Figure 7. Get your salesmen to complete as many forms as they can over that three-month period. Get them also to list business in order of potential—biggest first, smallest last.

You'll see that the form provides for breaking down each individual customer or prospect forecast into quarterly periods and according to the products involved. There is also a column for noting the minimum calls the salesman reckons he needs to allocate to each customer next year—another thing he could agree upon with the customer when asking those forecasting questions.

Having the "Minimum Calls" column next to the "Total

●SALES CONTROL & RECORD SYSTEMS LTD RSF SF2

LIST CUSTOMERS IN ORDER OF POTENTIAL, GREATEST FIRST **SALES FORECAST** for year _____ Salesman **J. WATSON** Sheet 1 of 4 Sheets

CUSTOMER	ACCOUNT CATEGORY	MINIMUM CALLS NEEDED IN YEAR	TOTAL FORECAST	FORECAST SPREAD				PRODUCT GROUP BREAKDOWN										
				FIRST QUARTER	SECOND QUARTER	THIRD QUARTER	FOURTH QUARTER	0	1	2	3	4	5	6	7	8	9
TOTALS BROUGHT FORWARD																	
EATON & Co	C	20	2,400	600	600	600	600	1800	600								
BLOGGS & SMALL	A	20	2,200	600	500	500	600				1000		600			600
BRT	C	20	2,000	600	400	500	500	2000								
V. BLAND	B	20	1,600	600	500		500	1000				600			
R. SYSON & Co	H	20	1,500	500		500	500		1500						
WILSON VALTON Int	A	10	1,300	800			500		800	500					
C.K. VALVES	D	20	1,300	400	300	300	300	800				500			
ALLAN & RICHARDS	D	6	1,200	800			400		1200						
G. & S. TUGEE	D	20	1,000	300	200	200	300					500	500		
TOBIN & Co	C	9	1,000	400	100		500		300	200			200	200	
BERRY METERS	F	9	950	300	250		400				950				
ALLSOP COMP'RS	D	9	950	350	200		450					550			400
POTTERSBY & Co	G	10	950	300	200	150	300		600	250					
BREEDON SMITH	G	9	900	300	300		300	300	200			200			
ASH & Co	A	6	900	450			450				450	450			
SUPER VALVE Co	G	7	900	400	100		400	500				400			
WEBSTER & BLACK	H	10	900	400	100	100	300	400				500			
WYMAN WELDING	B	20	800	200	200	200	200	400	400						
QUALITY ELECT.	A	6	800	400			400			800					
REDDITCH VALVES	D	6	800	400			400		800						
TOTALS CARRIED FORWARD		257	24,350	9,150	3,950	3,050	8,300	2,600	5,300	5,300	1650	2,400	3,200	2,200	700	400	600

●SALES CONTROL & RECORD SYSTEMS LTD RSF SF2

LIST CUSTOMERS IN ORDER OF POTENTIAL, GREATEST FIRST **SALES FORECAST** for year _____ Salesman **J. WATSON** Sheet 4 of 4 Sheets

CUSTOMER	ACCOUNT CATEGORY	MINIMUM CALLS NEEDED IN YEAR	TOTAL FORECAST	FORECAST SPREAD				PRODUCT GROUP BREAKDOWN										
				FIRST QUARTER	SECOND QUARTER	THIRD QUARTER	FOURTH QUARTER	0	1	2	3	4	5	6	7	8	9
TOTALS BROUGHT FORWARD		728	61,650	22,650	12,000	10,150	16,800	6,800	12,150	13,650	3,700	6,000	14,100	4,600	1,800	1,250	1,000
PNEUMATIC LOGIC	C	4	400	200			200	200	100				100		
DAVIS GEARING	C	4	400	100	100	100	100	200				200			
AUTOLIFT	B	5	350	150	50		150			150	100		100		
WHITACRE & MILBRO	G	6	250	100	50	50	150				250				
SEMELE ENG	E	3	300	100	100		100						100	100	100
ROCKY PRECISION	E	4	200	150			150					100	100		
APPLEGATE & Co	A	6	300	100	50	50	100		100			100	100		
FRANCIS BERWICK	E	3	250	100		50	100	250							
WAKEFIELDS	C	4	250	150	50		50	100				100	50		
AP MOTORS	F	3	200	100		50	50	100	50	50					
GENERAL ELECTRIC	F	4	200	50	50	50	50		100		100				
NORTH & TIPPETT	E	2	200	100			100		100			50	50		
TOTALS CARRIED FORWARD		776	65,150	24,050	12,500	10,500	18,100	7,250	14,150	13,600	4,100	6,000	10,900	5,600	2,150	1,500	1,100

Figure 7. Sales forecast forms, sheets 1 and 4.

Forecast" column wasn't just an accident. You know how many calls each of your salesmen are likely to be able to make during the next year. So count up the calls allocated in the "Minimum Calls" column, from the top of the first sheet, until you arrive at the total calls possible in the year. Draw a line across the Forecast sheet at that point. Then add up the business in the "Total Forecast" column from the top of sheet one until you get to the line. That's the total amount of business this salesman has got time to get, if you accept his minimum call figures.

You now have a superb starting point from which to determine, by agreement, the salesman's final sales target for next year. Bring in his personal performance ratios, which are detailed in the section entitled "Personal Performance," and you have everything you need to get the very best out of every salesman.

TOTAL FORECAST

When you have established the sales target for each salesman, if these targets are still in the same format as the original forecasts—which they should be—you can total them up on a card like the one shown in Figure 8 and produce a total company forecast which should keep production, finance, and everyone else happy—as long as you achieve it, of course.

This system of forecasting doesn't suit *every* type of business, only MOST kinds, but the principles can be used, even in cases where 90 percent of your business is "contract" or "one-of-a-kind."

Growth

Every company needs growth; otherwise, it dies very quickly or is devoured by its competitors.

*SALES CONTROL & RECORD SYSTEMS LTD.

REF. MRS

SALES FORECAST - USERS & KNOWN PROSPECTS   YEAR _____

SALESMAN	MINIMUM CALLS NEEDED IN YEAR	TOTAL FORECAST	FORECAST SPREAD				TURNOVER EXPECTED FROM EACH PRODUCT GROUP									
			FIRST QUARTER	SECOND QUARTER	THIRD QUARTER	FOURTH QUARTER	0	1	2	3	4	5	6	7	8	9
1 J. Watson	776															
2 C. Briggs																
3 L. Sutton																
4 F. Winters																
5 G. Hopkins																
6 A. Rouse																
7 B. Smith																
8 S. Armstrong																
9 T. Jones																
10 V. Asworth																
11																
12																
13																
14																
15																
16																
17																
18																
19																
20																
21																
22																
23																
24																
25																
TOTALS																

Figure 8. Total company forecast form.

There are four ways for the average company to secure growth:

1. Increase its share of existing markets with its existing products, normally at the expense of its competitors (*market penetration*).
2. Find and develop *new* markets for its existing products (*market development*).
3. Develop *new* products which can be sold to existing markets (*product development*).
4. *Diversification*—usually by acquisition.

Most sales managers are concerned mainly with 1 and 2. Some take partial interest in 3. Few get involved in 4—that's left to the board of directors. (But who makes recommendations to the board, and on what criteria do acquisitions take place?)

Growth is *not* achieved by simply increasing prices, or by maintaining one's market share in an expanding market. Yet many practicing managers still fall into these traps, and think things are going well when they are really losing ground rapidly.

THE FIVE-YEAR PLAN

Not long ago, I came upon a company—well-respected in its field—that had just put the finishing touches on its next five-year plan.

Turnover projections were based on an objective of approximately 25 percent growth per year over the five years. Current turnover was $1,000,000, and the projection looked like this:

First year turnover	$1,000,000
Second year turnover	$1,250,000
Third year turnover	$1,600,000
Fourth year turnover	$1,950,000

| Fifth year turnover | $2,500,000 |
| Sixth year turnover | $3,000,000 |

A new factory extension was allowed for in the plan to cope with future production, but there was no provision whatever for new product development. And, apart from plans to increase the secretarial staff of the sales office at strategic points along the turnover progression, the only other consideration given to the sales operation's part in this planned expansion was to budget for the employment of one extra salesman for every $200,000 increment of new turnover. The $200,000 figure was decided on because the average turnover currently achieved by each of the existing salesmen was between $160,000 and $200,000 per year.

The executives of this particular company were happily looking forward to the next five years, and were content with the projected profit margins. They saw no insurmountable problems in finding the necessary number of new salesmen and training them up to effectiveness. They saw no shortfall developing in the market potential, or delays through any failure to win shares of business from the competitors. They had even allowed for the costs of replacing some of their salesmen who might leave during the five-year period.

So when I suggested to these executives that the projected turnover could be achieved *without* the need to increase the size of the present sales force by even one man, you can in all probability imagine the cynical smiles I received. ("Humor him and he'll go away," etc.)

At least they gave me the opportunity to show them what I was thinking. "*If* prices increase 10 percent a year during this next five years, what increase in turnover will this give the company without any other finger needed to be lifted?" The answer:

| First year | $1,000,000 |
| Second year | $1,100,000 |

Third year	$1,210,000
Fourth year	$1,331,000
Fifth year	$1,464,000
Sixth year	$1,610,000

"So you're a significant way toward your five-year target on straight price increases alone," I said.

Next question: "What kind of personal development program have you got for your salesmen?"

This question was greeted by a somewhat puzzled, "What do you mean?" "Well," I replied, "if your salesmen are pulling in $200,000 worth of business this year, what scope are you going to give them for expanding on this? What encouragement for them to attain $250,000 next year? What back-up to make this attainment easier? What extra rewards if they move on to $300,000? What ongoing training to develop their knowledge of the products, the applications for the products, and the markets for these applications?

"If your salesmen continue to pull in just $160,000 to $200,000 worth of business a year," I continued, "how long will it be, do you think, before they get fed up, lose that all-important job satisfaction, reckon they're in a rut and not getting anywhere—and quit?"

The puzzled frowns gradually turned to genuine surprise.

I rubbed some salt into the wound: "To lose a good salesman and have to replace him at short notice would cost the company several months' new business turnover, the loss of good-will, plus about $10,000 to train the new man up to full effectiveness. Even then, there would be some uncertainty—whether or not the new salesman will make the grade, and the cost of having to start all over again if he fails to make it."

Their surprise was changing to a certain amount of apprehension.

"Wouldn't it be much more sensible to have some kind of planned personal development program for each salesman, so that each man can develop his knowledge, his abilities, his territory, his customers, his sense of importance, his rewards based upon his own achievements—all this giving him the job satisfaction and pride that will keep him working effectively for you for many years to come?"

Nods and raised eyebrows.

"If, for example, each salesman could increase his turnover by 15 percent per year—in true terms, price increases excluded—and if he were to be rewarded accordingly in addition to his usual salary increases linked to the cost-of-living index, do you think this would provide him with some significant job satisfaction?"

Emphatic affirmatives. "More than some of 'em are worth," commented several executives.

"So how does this 15 percent personal improvement target linked to your calculated 10 percent price increases per year, influence your five-year turnover projection?"

The answer, of course, is obvious. The company could reach its $3 million target with no additional salesmen, and with much less risk of losing the salesmen it already employed. Profits significantly increased. Problems significantly reduced.

The five-year plan was amended forthwith.

WILL THE SALESMEN DO IT ON THEIR OWN?

It wouldn't have been fair to leave those directors with their revised five-year plan, just at that stage. So a few more questions were submitted.

"Would you have confidence in your present sales force's achieving a 15 percent annual increase in true turnover on its own—without supervision, without encouragement, without help, or without your at least monitoring the results as they happen?"

Heavy signs. "I thought it would be too good to be true," some say.

"So how are you going to make sure it all happens? How are you going to monitor and measure your salesmen's performance as the months and the years go by, to make sure the desired improvement is achieved? How are you going to establish what back-up is necessary, and in what area of the country, or in what sector of the market or section of the product range? How are you going to calculate the amount of advertising and sales promotion required in each territory, to generate the kind of response each salesman needs in order to make his "new business" target attainable without tears or frustration, or weeks of door-knocking? How are you going to make sure each salesman does the selling part of his job as effectively as possible, and the planning part of his job as efficiently as possible? How are you going to pinpoint problems in any salesman's effectiveness, quickly—so that you can rectify the problems just as quickly and stay on target? How are you going to get the salesmen to monitor their own territories so that they keep you fully aware of how the market is doing so that you don't miss out on any potential business?"

Hands in the air. "Stop, stop. We haven't the time to do all that," the executives say. "Our sales manager can't even spare the time to get out in the field with his salesmen more than once or twice a month. He's already inundated with more paperwork than he can handle."

"But does the paperwork he handles at present give him all the information I have just mentioned? And in a form which makes it easy to use? If his reporting and control system is really working for him, it shouldn't need to take more than one hour a week of his time. My guess is that most of the paperwork with which he gets loaded at present isn't really necessary, or doesn't really do the job it was intended to do.

"Most sales forces will not achieve any meaningful improvement in performance on their own. In fact, the reverse is true. Left to their own devices, most salesmen will gradually decline in performance. Every sales force needs a strong, determined, dedicated, enthusiastic sales manager. A leader. A manager who really manages. A man who can achieve results through the efforts of other people—his team. Not a promoted salesman who still thinks of himself as a salesman.

"And that sales manager, that team leader, must have at his fingertips all the information, figures, ratios, and statistics that will enable him to plan his next move, and the shape of the improvement target for each individual salesman in his team."

"What kind of information?" the directors demanded.

1. How many days a year are available to the sales force for actual selling?
2. How many face-to-face calls can they make?
3. Which existing customers are worth calling on in the next year, which ones are not, and why?
4. How much business will each of these existing customers produce next year?
5. How many calls will the sales force need to make to secure this repeat business?
6. How much time does the sales force have available to seek *new* business?
7. What proportion of the total business comes from quotations?
8. What is the conversion ratio of quotations into orders?
9. What is the average order value for (*a*) repeat business, and (*b*) new business?
10. How many quotations must be generated to get to target?
11. What is each salesman's average miles per call ratio?
12. How many of each salesman's calls are made by appointment?

After an hour's discussion and quite a few internal telephone calls, the directors had to admit that their company could make a reasonable guess at four of these twelve questions, but only a guess. No one was actually recording any data

from which a precise figure could be derived. This appeared to
worry them.

"You have a significant element of Fudge Factor in your
sales operation," I stated.

"Fudge Factor?" the directors chorused. "Fudge Factor?
What do you mean by that?"

FUDGE FACTOR

"Fudge Factor," I submitted, "is the result of management
not insisting on the sales force's accepting and working to the
same kind of disciplines expected of production, accounts,
transport, and most other departments in the company."

Fudge Factor is a term coined by Philip Lund, author of
Compelling Selling and *Sales Reports, Records and Systems.*
Lund's words on the subject are as follows.

*I have always found it hard to understand why people who
run successful businesses consistently allow themselves to be
betrayed by their field sales forces. For some strange reason,
these otherwise competent executives accept a level of fudge
factor from their sales operation that they would not tolerate
from the other departments of their business.*

*In sales planning, targets and performance can be quantified
and controls can be exercised through numbers just as easily as
they can in production or in management accounting. The
problem most businesses have had in the past, however, has
been to discard existing outdated sales procedures and to replace them without disruption by a complete, yet simple, system that would rationalize their sales planning and control
requirements.*

*No sales control system can replace the function of good field
sales management, of course, but with the right system, this
management will undoubtedly become much more efficient.*

As with most managements struggling to see the light for the
first time, a few comparisons had to be made to emphasize the

fact that Fudge Factor existed, and ran rampant through their organization.

"Let's look at Customer Records," I suggested. "Would you allow your accountant to jot down his accounts in a little black book and take them with him when he leaves your employment?

"Would you allow your production blue prints to be just casual sketches, and again taken away to another company when an engineer leaves?

"So what happens when one of your salesmen leaves? Before he goes, do you get back all his records and personal information on the customers and prospects in his territory? And if you do, are these records such that you can give them to his successor so that the new man can get his teeth into the job with the minimum of disruption of your sales effort?

"In fact, do you actually have a standard customer record system which you provide for your salesmen, or do you expect each man to devise and operate his own system?"

The silence was deafening.

"Let's look at Forward Planning," I continued.

"Do you demand from your accounts department a financial plan that enables the company to maintain adequate cash flow?

"Do you expect production to know what they are going to produce next week?

"Do you allow your delivery vans to go where they please?

"So do you get from your salesmen a plan of where they intend to go next week? And, more important, what they intend to do when they get there?

"Production knows its capacity, yet how many of your salesmen have worked out their *order capacity* for the next 12 months?

"If I may add a question on quality control. . . .

"Doubtless you take note of the amount of wastage of materials in your factory, and of the number of rejects and the scrap rates. Your accounts department is also keeping a close watch on all outstanding invoices, to make sure every customer pays his bills within a reasonable time. All the products in the factory are subjected to strict quality control and testing.

"But to what extent does your sales manager measure, inspect, and test the quality of his salesmen's performance?"

"Enough!" cried the executives. "What do you suggest we do?"

"Well, the first thing to do," I replied, "is to try to establish the extent to which Fudge Factor has taken a grip on your sales organization."

I handed each director a checklist. "Answer the 18 questions (listed below), and then let's see what we can do to rectify all the 'nos,' " I said. You can do the same for your organization by checking the appropriate column.

		Yes	No
1.	Do you provide your salesmen a standardized method for keeping customer records?	☐	☐
2.	Do your salesmen keep their customer records up to date—and *use* them?	☐	☐
3.	Do you make sure a salesman who leaves the company doesn't take his customer records with him?	☐	☐
4.	Do you know how much prospecting work your salesmen need to do to achieve the company's "New Business" target?	☐	☐
5.	If you can answer "Yes" to question 4, do you know if your salesmen are actually *doing* the amount of prospecting work required?	☐	☐
6.	Do you receive a detailed plan from your salesmen of where they will be next week?	☐	☐
7.	Are more than 40 percent of your salesmen's calls "By Appointment"?	☐	☐

	Yes	No
8. Do you know how much business your salesmen are chasing that your company has quoted for?	☐	☐
9. Do you know how much of this business is likely to result in firm orders *next month*?	☐	☐
10. Do your salesmen prepare for you a forecast of how much business they reckon they will produce for the company during the next period?	☐	☐
11. Is this forecast in a sufficiently detailed form so that you can pinpoint any specific customer that isn't coming up to expectations?	☐	☐
12. Are the Action Reports you receive from your salesmen sufficiently legible, detailed, and accurate for the company to produce a quotation and be certain it will fulfill the customer's requirements?	☐	☐
13. Do your salesmen submit a Weekly Report of the customers they have called upon—and what happened?	☐	☐
14. If the answer to question 13 is "Yes," does anyone use the information on the Weekly Reports, rather than just file them away after a general check?	☐	☐
15. Do you know if any salesmen are neglecting part of your product range?	☐	☐
16. Do you know your company's average order value?	☐	☐
17. Do you know your company's "calls to quotations" ratio?	☐	☐
18. Do you know your company's "quotations to orders" ratio?	☐	☐
Totals	☐	☐

Any reader who logs more than six "nos" on this checklist has a few major problems to solve. Read the section on "Personal Performance" to find out how to start measuring all these things with a minimum of paperwork and time commitment.

Holes (Sudden)

One of the biggest problems a sales manager faces is having one of his salesmen suddenly quit without warning, leaving him with a large hole which has to be filled before customer service suffers too much.

Only the largest companies can afford to take on one or two young trainees and to develop their potential in the sales office, waiting for a sudden hole to appear. Most sales managers have to draft a quick advertisement and hope for the best.

Two things you can do to reduce the problem:

1. Do some regular detective work and build up a file of personal contacts who might make good salesmen if and when the need arises. These might be salesmen working for other companies (but please, not your direct competitors) or even a few of your customers who yearn for the outdoor life and have the requisite temperament, abilities, and motivation. Then just a phone call would get you the new man you need.

2. Hold regular meetings with the other department heads in your company, and try to establish a procedure for growing your own new salesmen, fertilizing them (covering their costs) through the jobs they are doing in the other departments of the company. The one factor militating against this, of course,

is the sudden hole a man leaves in another department when he moves to sales. But holes in design, production, commercial, service, etc., are usually easier to fill or patch over than holes in sales.

If in Doubt—Ask

Just about every sheet of drawing paper used in every drawing office has these words printed on it in large letters: IF IN DOUBT—ASK.

No designer or engineer would ever dream of committing himself to something of a technical nature unless he was sure. So why doesn't the same principle apply to the sales office?

Half the quotations sent to customers by suppliers are inaccurate in some way, mainly because the instructions received from the salesman were incomplete or illegible.

And rarely, if ever, does the sales office throw the instruction back at the salesman and ask him to do it again, or fill in the gaps. Instead, the sales office tries to interpret the instructions as best it can.

And another potential order is lost.

Make your sales office different. Make everyone operate under those fundamental words on the drawing paper: IF IN DOUBT—ASK.

Make it easy for your salesmen to provide the information the sales office needs. Get the salesmen using checklists and properly designed forms for their action requests, like the one shown in Figure 9.

And give your sales office manager the authority to send things back to the salesmen, and tell them to do the job properly. The problem will soon disappear.

ACTION REQUEST   SALESMAN *J. Watson*

COMPANY'S FULL NAME	DATE OF CALL
R.K. Valves, Inc.	

FULL ADDRESS INCL. POSTAL CODE
**3343 Maiden Lane
Anytown, U.S.A. 12345**

CONTACT'S NAME AND INITIALS
W.F. Evans
POSITION IN COMPANY
Asst. Plant Buyers

Please Requote on basis of our Quote No. 4267 (RT) of July 17th, but Provide for:

(A) Multi-Spindle Attachment (J7A)

(B) Double set of Tools and 2 Spares Kits.

(C) Provide for estimated price increases by March next year (date of client's decision to Purchase).

COMPETITION
All usual **U.S.** Companies plus Speigel GmbH, Essen, Germany

ANYTHING ATTACHED   **No**

ACTION   Vital before October 31st (Board Meeting of Client will decide first sorting of tenders on Nov. 2)

DEADLINE   Oct. 31st

SEND EVERYTHING TO THE SALESMAN	SEND DIRECT TO THE CONTACT NAMED ABOVE X	HQ REPLY TO SALESMAN IF PROBLEMS FAST

© SALES CONTROL & RECORD SYSTEMS LTD.   REF AR

Figure 9.   Action request form.

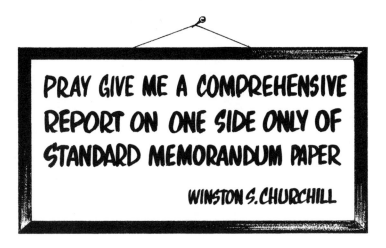

PRAY GIVE ME A COMPREHENSIVE
REPORT ON ONE SIDE ONLY OF
STANDARD MEMORANDUM PAPER

WINSTON S. CHURCHILL

Interdepartmental Relationships

Most companies have more problems communicating among their own departments than they do communicating with their customers and suppliers. Probably it's because so much is taken for granted by so many.

If you want to have some fun and at the same time get your interdepartmental communications straightened out, circulate the checklist shown in Figure 10 to all department heads, with a memo saying: "Please, can we discuss your findings on the attached checklist at our next monthly management meeting?"

You'll find at·the next meeting that everyone has blamed everyone else. Let the discussion rage for half an hour, and then quietly ask everyone at the meeting to reflect on the past 30 minutes. You'll have to take some of the blame, of course—just like the others.

	N/A	YES	NO	PAR	?	ACT
1. In relation to other departments which of the following are causing delays or problems in my departments and should be discussed at management meetings?						
(a) Relevant information not being transmitted by other departments?						
(b) Incomplete information received from other departments?						
(c) Work flow interruptions caused by constant requests for immediate action or information?						
(d) Formal lines of communication being ignored or by-passed?						
(e) Verbal communications lacking in clarity — resulting in misunderstandings and misinterpretation?						
(f) Requests for action/information not complied with?						
(g) Impaired efficiency due to forgetfulness by other departments?						
(h) A build up of frustration caused by poor communications between departments?						
2. If I prepare specific recommendations on ways and means to improve any of the above are they likely to be accepted and complied with?						
3. If 'No' or 'Query', can I indicate the loss of efficiency caused by any particular shortcoming(s)?						
4. .... and thus gain acceptance and co-operation?						
5. Have we recently studied our methods and lines of communications and assessed the present weaknesses in relation to future expansion?						
6. If no, should we seek suggestions from departments upon improvements or communications?						
7. .... or hold a meeting to discuss the present deficiencies?						
8. Is any one person or department persistently lacking in good communications?						
9. If yes, have they been made fully aware of the problems that are being created?						
10. Are we inclined to rely too heavily upon verbal communications?						
11. If yes, should we assess which verbal communications are frequently inadequate?						
12. .... and apply written communications to overcome this?						
13. Have we studied which repetitive communications affect more than one person or department?						
14. .... and considered the simplest and quickest method of imparting the information to all concerned?						
15. Could important requests and replies be conveyed via internal memo's?						
16. .... which also indicate the degree of urgency?						
17. .... supported by a 'bring-up' procedure for those requests which require acknowledgement, answer or action?						
18. Are documents date-stamped by departments to show dates of receipt and completion?						
19. .... to indicate the total time taken to process.						
20. Are documents coded to indicate the degree of priority?						
21. .... and the need for feed-back information?						
22. Is the principal of 'do it now' sufficiently instilled in Managers and staff?						

Figure 10. Checklist on communications.

Job Specifications and Job Descriptions

Would you believe that the majority of people in selling and sales management don't have either?

A job description is like a compass—it points you in the right direction and keeps you there. Try steering a ship without a compass.

Any sales manager without a job description should at once set about writing his own, then submit it to the powers that be for approval, or modification and then approval.

A sales manager taking on new salesmen begins with a job specification—a negotiating document used to make sure the applicant fits all the key tasks required of him, or at least most of them. Once taken on, this job specification is redrafted to include the specific detail on individual performance standards expected and then becomes that individual applicant's job description.

If a sales manager has to draft job descriptions from scratch for an existing sales force, the best method is to get every salesman to draft his own, then pool the results and have the sales manager himself develop the final format and the individual detailed contents for each salesman.

SAMPLE JOB SPECIFICATION FOR A SALESMAN

Job Title: Sales Manager
Responsible to: West Coast Sales Manager
Sales Area: The Sales Area Known as Area Number 5
Purpose: To maintain and develop business with existing customers in the area and to develop business by locating and selling to new outlets in the area.

Prime Duties and Responsibilities:

1. To acquire a thorough working knowledge of all the company's products and a thorough understanding of all their applications.

To keep this knowledge up to date through regular sales meetings and product training sessions held monthly at headquarters.

Performance will be considered satisfactory when full selling proposals, including detailed financial justification, can be drafted for all customer applications to be found in Area Number 5.

2. To acquire and develop all necessary professional selling skills through the meetings and training sessions referred to in 1, through attendance at outside sales training courses in accordance with the company's personal development programs, and by discussion, reading, and constant practice.

Performance will be considered satisfactory when all eight personal performance ratios are consistently better than the company norms for these ratios, and all factors on the monthly personal selling standards record are consistently marked "above standard."

3. To plan the coverage of the area in the most effective and economic manner.

Performance will be considered satisfactory when:

(*a*) All customer and prospective customer records are up to date and contain full information on names, initials, and positions of all contacts, the best day and time to call on each contact, the name of the secretary, as well as a properly reported call record which specifies in all cases the aim of the *next* call and the firm date of the next call.

(*b*) These customer and prospective customer records can be used to produce a forecast of future business expected from the area, which is subsequently proved accurate.

(c) A cycle-of-calling plan is in existence for the area and is being worked in a systematic manner.

(d) A list of live new business prospects is being properly researched every month, prior to calling, and the number of prospects on each monthly list is consistent with the known requirement for that time which has been calculated from the personal performance ratios.

(e) At all times there is an adequate list of prospects in negotiation, and steady movement toward conclusion can be demonstrated.

(f) A fully detailed call plan, itemizing all calls to be made during the following week and with at least 60 percent of these calls having firm appointments, is received every Friday by the West Coast sales manager.

4. To report coherently and with speed and economy of words on day-to-day activities, customer installations, prevailing or changing business trends, customer complaints and satisfaction, and competitors' activity, such reporting to be in accordance with directives issued from time to time by the sales manager and on the appropriate forms supplied for these purposes.

5. Attendance at all regional sales meetings, national sales meetings, and company-organized training sessions is mandatory.

6. To liaise whenever necessary with the sales office manager, chief engineer, development manager, production manager, and chief accountant to ensure that a proper level of customer service and customer advice is maintained.

7. To develop relationships with customers that further the goodwill connected with the company name.

Performance in this respect will be considered satisfactory when sales demonstrations to prospects take place at existing customers' premises in the area on a regular basis and the reception given to company personnel when visiting customers in the area is seen generally to reflect this goodwill.

8. The prime objective will be met when sales in the area by total, rate, and product mix equate with the forecasts prepared for and the targets set for the area.

SAMPLE JOB SPECIFICATION FOR A SALES MANAGER

Job Title:	U.S. Sales Manager
Responsible to:	CEO or President (this sample assumes the company has no sales or marketing activity)
Responsible for:	All U.S. Sales activities
Staff Responsible for:	All U.S. Sales Engineers
	Sales Office Manager
	Service Manager
	Product Managers (if any)
	Technical Services Manager
	Marketing Services (Including Publicity)
Main Purpose of Job:	To control and coordinate the U.S. sales and marketing activities of the company, based at the company's head office, and to ensure the highest possible profitability at the correct balance of product sales, the efficient operation of the sales department, and maximum job satisfaction for the personnel employed therein and for whom the U.S. sales manager is directly responsible.

Main Duties and Responsibilities:

1. To advise the board of directors on all matters of policy relating to U.S. sales and marketing.

2. To direct and manage the sales department within the policies laid down by the board of directors.

3. To liaise with the export sales manager on use of the technical services department and the marketing services department for export activities.

4. To liaise with product managers and to discuss, agree on, and implement variations in product sales policies whenever deemed necessary.

5. To arbitrate on all serious disagreements with customers, if necessary enlisting the CEO's help, and to bring all such disagreements to the speediest possible conclusion that is satisfactory to the customer.

6. In conjunction with the board of directors and the personnel manager, to establish salary and commission formulas to meet the needs of the sales personnel, bearing in mind the objective of matching maximum profitability to maximum job satisfaction.

7. To prepare and submit to the board of directors the annual and long-range expenditure and capital budgets for those departments for which the sales manager is responsible, and likewise all sales forecasts relating to annual and long-range product sales.

8. To monitor continuously actual costs against budgeted costs, and actual sales against budgeted sales for the U.S. sales operation.

9. To ensure that a congenial working environment is maintained within all departments for which the sales manager is responsible.

10. To undertake all interviews and selection of new staff for the sales force.

11. To ensure that all employees for whom the sales manager is responsible receive adequate training to fit them for the jobs they are employed to do.

12. To chair all product planning meetings.

13. To direct and control U.S. product strategy.

14. To direct and control U.S. marketing strategy.
15. To control product mix with appropriate liaison with the production manager and with regard to the objective of maximum profitability.
16. To prepare a monthly report on U.S. sales activity for the board of directors.
17. To spend at least one day per month in the field with each of the sales engineers, to assess the sales engineer's performance and progress, and to give any assistance necessary to assure steady progress.
18. To monitor U.S. sales activities and assure that satisfactory performance levels are maintained for the sales force as a whole and for each sales engineer individually.
19. To recommend and implement changes in manpower structure and control where necessary within the U.S. sales operation.
20. To ensure that effective disciplinary procedures are in force and carried out within the U.S. sales operation.
21. To carry out such additional duties as may become necessary from time to time to ensure the smooth running of the U.S. sales operation.

As you can probably see, the sales manager's job *specification* is a shady more "all-enveloping" than the salesman's. There are so many varieties of sales managers that it is impossible to standardize. Thus, my sample is for guideline purposes only. Here is part of a sales manager's detailed job *description*, listing his performance standards.

Just for the sales manager who is faced with the task of selling the concept of job specifications and descriptions to his president or CEO, here is a sample for a chief executive.

JOB DESCRIPTION: Sales manager

REPORTS TO: CEO, President, or Vice-President, Marketing.

MAIN RESPONSIBILITY: The attainment of sales objectives through the effective operation of the field sales force.

SALES OBJECTIVES:

Organizes, leads, trains, motivates, and controls the sales force to ensure the on-time attainment of sales objectives, and in particular, the attainment of:

1. Sales targets by product.
2. Sales targets by territory.
3. Sales targets by key customers.
4. Sales activity by region.
5. Sales activity by territory.

Standards of performance relative to the above are attained when:

1. The national annual sales target is attained.
2. The number of salesmen not attaining target is below 15 percent of the field force.
3. More than 80 percent of the key accounts have attained or surpassed the agreed-on target figure.
4. The national average effective call rate is 6 per man per day.
5. The inquiry-to-call ratio is less than 1:7 and is seen to be declining.
6. The number of product demonstrations averages at least 3 per man per day.
7. When the number of "orders on the spot" averages at least 5 per man per week, and is increasing.
8. When the order-to-call ratio is less than 1:8 and is declining.
9. When the order-to-inquiry ratio is less than 1:1.5.
10. When the average value of order is $500 and increasing.
11. When the number of calls made on new prospects averages at least 5 per man per week.
12. When the number of calls made upon dormant accounts averages at least 2 per man per week.
13. When the cost per call is less than $50.
14. When the average gross margin is held to 15 percent.
15. When the direct sales cost is held at or below 12.5 percent.

SAMPLE JOB SPECIFICATION FOR A
CHIEF EXECUTIVE

Job Title:	Chief Executive
	American Widgets, Inc.
Reporting to:	Vice-President, Marketing
	Universal Widget Corpora-
	tion
Liaison with:	Moulded Widgets, Inc.
	(Chief Executive)
	Widgets SA France (Manag-
	ing Director)
	Widgets Gmbh (Managing
	Director)
Function:	Overall responsibility for the
	profitable management of
	American Widgets, Inc.
Geographic Area:	United States
Group Management Meetings:	Attendance at monthly
	management meetings with
	associate group companies
	is mandatory.

Duties:
1. *Marketing*
- To achieve a high market share in volume and value.
- To maximize price levels consistent with market share and volume.
- To appraise constantly and to update marketing policies.
- To review economic data relevant to markets on a consistent basis.
- To review market trends, competitive activity, and general market data.
- To develop and update all advertising, promotional activities, and product literature.
- To maintain customer service in respect of sales adminis-

tration, distribution stocks, and spare inventory, relative to sales forecasts.
- To develop sound relationships with relevant trade associations and professional and technical bodies operating in the United States.
- To develop sales for present products in new markets.
- To obtain and maintain a wide range of live business contacts.
- To provide vigor in the sales force.

2. *Financial*
- To ensure that all company activities are coordinated by the Financial Controller and that all reports and returns required by company law are filed in due time.
- To maintain under strict surveillance all cost/profit contributions on a regular basis.
- To keep a watching brief on cost trends.
- To control and anticipate overhead expenses using planned budgets.
- To ensure that all costing systems have instant update.
- To review debtors on a minimum monthly basis.
- To control inventory levels.
- To provide adequate space for planned inventory.
- To shed unprofitable products.
- To maintain the group's price leadership philosophy.
- To produce all necessary budgets and forecasts.

3. *Production/Product Development*
- To maintain and enhance product quality.
- To ensure that production units (own and sub-contract) have sales forecasts.
- To maintain a review of end users and specifiers of Widgets in all markets.
- To improve present range of products.
- To develop a more effective product mix.

- To develop a more effective market mix.
- To develop new products for new markets.
- To coordinate existing products and new products.

4. To ensure that a monthly report covering Marketing, Finance, and Production/Product Development is submitted to the Vice-President, Marketing.

5. *Purchasing*
   To ensure that products and materials required for American Widgets, Inc., are procured from reliable, cost-effective, and technically competent sources.

6. *Personnel*
   - To recruit management personnel and to delegate to them duties as required.
   - To attract to and maintain at American Widgets, Inc., top-quality management and staff.
   - To remunerate and motivate above-average people at above-average levels as an investment in long-term performance.
   - To develop future managers for expanding operations elsewhere in Universal Widget Corporation.
   - To maintain a good working environment.
   - To update terms and conditions of employment in line with current legislation.
   - To develop on a continuous basis an improved organizational structure.

7. *Legal*
   - To take appropriate legal advice on all relevant matters, and to refer to fellow directors and Vice-President, Marketing on these relevant matters.
   - To be watchful and defensive of the company's patents, registered designs, copyrights, and trade names.

- To maintain a strictly legal posture in dealing with employees, suppliers, customers, unions, local authorities, and government departments.

8. *Planning*
- To ensure that adequate medium and long-range plans are produced for products in:
  (a) the motor vehicle widget market
  (b) the aerospace widget market
  (c) the civil engineering widget market
- To perceive new needs and opportunities and to prepare and submit plans accordingly to the Vice-President, Marketing.

Chief executives who also perform the function of Sales Manager need to knit these two sample job specifications together to make one. You want any better reason to start looking for a sales manager? It's better than getting a coronary!

Key Questions for Sales Managers

> *I have six honest serving men*
> *They taught me all I know.*
> *Their names are What and Why and*
> *When*
> *Where and How and Who.*
> > KIPLING

WHAT?

What are my own personal objectives?
What do I want to accomplish in life?
What personal results am I trying to achieve?
For what purpose?

WHY?

Why am I striving to do this?
Why is it necessary?
Does it have permanent value?
Temporary value?
Is it 100 percent useful?

WHEN?

When is this going to be accomplished?
Long-range? Short-range?
What's the schedule?

WHERE?

Where have I been?
Where am I now?
Where am I going from here?

HOW?

How am I going to accomplish my major objectives?
How can I improve my present performance?

WHO?

Who are my most helpful advisers?
And critics?
Who should be consulted about what problems?
Who is best qualified to do what?
Who are the outstanding leaders in my field?

Leadership

This is the most important quality of all for a sales manager. It is very difficult to define. Some people have it from childhood; others have to work very hard at the main ingredients that make a good leader of salesmen.

Here is a work list for the hard working:

1. *A good memory.* This will enable him to recall people's names, and the few essential facts that are pertinent to a wide range of problems.

2. *A genuine interest in people.* Those whom you are responsible for leading will know at once if you are genuinely interested in them and particularly in their development. Show this and you create the personal bond that is essential to the success of your team. You *cannot* fake an interest in people; they *always* find you out.

A leader can only be successful by ensuring the success of every individual in the team.

3. *Integrity.* If the team has cause to doubt the integrity of its leader, then it will fail when the team is exposed to stress or a risk.

If a man is capable of minor lapses in his personal integrity (if he fails to "keep faith"), then he could let his own team members down when he is under pressure. Once the team members doubt the leader, that doubt greatly limits their chances of the fullest success.

4. *The ability to communicate effectively.* A good leader must be able to talk—and write—simply, clearly, and persuasively. He must also listen—and digest information—intently. Communication is a two-way process.

5. *Decisiveness.* There comes a time when a decision must be made and a risk taken, even though the facts may be incomplete.

A leader must recognize when further analysis is unprofitable and action is needed.

It helps if the cost of changing the decision is known. If the cost is low, the risk is low.

6. *The ability to relax.* If the team is kept tense and under pressure, irritation arises and performance fails. This is overcome by deliberately introducing a "break"—a light remark or opportunity for laughter.

The importance lies in the frequency and the need for the "break" to be related to the task or the people—not just a "funny story." The break should be brief, even momentary. It should also come at an opportune moment.

7. *Genuine enthusiasm.* Inner conviction—belief in the team and in its objectives—gives rise to enthusiasm. This *must* be visible to the members of the team. It provides the motive power they use to tackle their jobs with courage and hope.

If the leader has no belief in the task, why should his team even attempt it?

League Standings

Don't ever try to hide the company's true performance from your salesmen or disguise money figures by allocating code numbers or units. Play it all straight; tell everyone the worst—and the best.

Give each salesman a detailed rundown of his sales figures, calls, quotations, leads, ratios, profitability, and whatever, at least once a month. Give each salesman everyone else's figures also. Let everyone see how everyone else is doing.

Only then will you begin to convert the salesmen at the bottom of the league standings into self-starters. All you need to do after that is keep filling the tank and priming the gas pump.

The best kind of league standings is one which relates to the annual targets, and which allows the targets to be adjusted as the months progress (not the targets related to commission earnings). Figure 11 shows one example, for a company employing twenty salesmen and having four area sales managers who regularly reassess the business outlook for each of their salesmen.

SALESMAN	RESULTS AT END OF MONTH – 8			AREA MANAGER'S CURRENT ESTIMATE FOR REST OF YEAR		
	ORIGINAL AGREED ANNUAL TARGET	TURNOVER ACHIEVED SO FAR	BALANCE LEFT TO ACHIEVE	WILL MAKE BALANCE ON NOSE	WILL SELL MORE THAN BALANCE BY	WILL SELL LESS THAN BALANCE BY
ANDREWS, J.	150,000	98,000	52,000	✓		
ARNOLD, P.	150,000	122,000	28,000	✓		
BEASLEY, G.	110,000	108,000	2,000		25,000	
BREWSTER, M	110,000	85,000	25,000	✓		
CARVER, D.	84,000	61,000	23,000	✓		
EVANS, D.	110,000	73,000	37,000			20,000
GILLMAN, R.	140,000	80,000	60,000			25,000
JACOBS, E.	125,000	123,000	2,000		35,000	
KEITH, B.	80,000	58,000	22,000		5,000	
McEWAN, J.	86,000	35,000	51,000			33,000
NORMAN, L.	150,000	105,000	45,000	✓		
ONIONS, P.	127,000	90,000	37,000			17,000
PACKER, A.	165,000	122,000	43,000		10,000	
PORTER, J.	130,000	70,000	60,000			30,000
ROBERTS, G.	55,000	36,000	19,000	✓		
SUTCLIFFE, S.	102,000	75,000	27,000			7,000
TAYLOR, B.	60,000	37,000	23,000		7,000	
THOMPSON, P.	110,000	79,000	31,000		2,000	
VINCENT, W.	100,000	85,000	15,000		18,000	
WATSON, J.	150,000	110,000	40,000		5,000	

All figures rounded up or down to nearest 1000.

Figure 11.   Table of league standings.

Low Potential Accounts

Eighty percent of your repeat business will be coming from less than 20 percent of your customers.

And 80 percent of your salesmen's time will be spent servicing customers who bring in less than 20 percent of the total repeat business, unless you mainly deal in "one-of-a-kinds."

These are facts of life—and facts that are quickly making the salesman a very expensive animal to have on the payroll.

It's a general dilemma right across industry. You cannot afford to allow your salesmen to call very often on low potential customers, and you cannot afford to lose that 20 percent of turnover, because some of today's small fry will be tomorrow's medium-size and big customers.

The answer to the dilemma is to service repeat business from your low potential accounts by telephone, not by salesmen. Put together a tele-sales desk at each of your regional offices (if you have any) or do it from the head office. (The cost of the telephone calls will still be much lower than the cost of face-to-face calls.)

The successful changeover from salesmen to telephone sales depends on your following these steps:

1. Tell your salesmen what you have in mind and why. Ask each of them to give you a list of the low potential customers whom they feel are suitable for the new tele-sales service. Impress upon the salesmen that no nasty or difficult customers should go on the list—only easy, happy ones. Also impress upon the salesmen that any time one of these customers wants to see a salesman, a salesman will be allowed to call.

2. Allocate specific customers to specific tele-sales staff. Make sure only the person allocated that customer ever telephones that customer, and then thoroughly train the staff in tele-sales techniques and how to start the ball rolling.

3. Send each customer a specially designed package of literature, product stock lists, price lists, etc., to introduce the new

tele-sales service, like the example from Herbert Tooling, Ltd. shown in Figure 12. Note carefully the text in this example.

4. Follow up the literature with the first telephone call a few days later. (A good tele-sales person never has a problem persuading even the most cynical and reluctant customer at least to give the new service a try. After all, he's got absolutely nothing to lose, or to do; all he can do is gain.)

AVAILABLE EQUIPMENT

The telephone company can make a tele-sales desk highly efficient. To back up the ordinary telephone there are a

The easiest ever method of ordering small tools

For some time now we have been operating what we firmly believe to be today's most efficient and trouble-free tool ordering service. We supply the widest range of small tools currently available, most of the time delivered within 48 hours. All that is needed from you is one phone call to your Herbert Distribution Centre.

Now we're taking the ultimate step. We've even managed to eliminate the phone call.

From now on we are offering to a carefully selected group of valued clients, a completely new ordering service. One which requires you to do nothing except answer the phone. Here's how it works.

After consultation with you, we will arrange to ring any number and extension you wish, talk to any individual you nominate at whatever times and on whatever dates you decide fits your system best.

We will contact you monthly, weekly, or whenever you like. We will call on a given day of the month, or on a selected day of the week. When we call, simply give us your order and the Herbert computerised ordering system will go into action, bringing your tools with the minimum of delay. Or you can simply say "Nothing today thanks!" and we'll ring off until next time.

Think of the advantages:
* No need to remember to ring us for tools.
* No chance of being held up by busy phone lines, or the vagaries of the post office.
* Constant communication with the most efficient tool service in Britain. With no effort from yourself.
* And a corresponding reduction in your phone bill.

To enjoy this service you need take no action. In a few days we will ring you to see if we can be of service.

If after due consideration you decide that this new service is not for you – tell us on our next call and we won't bother you with it again.

One last thing – if you join the 'Phone-in' service or not, you can always get top Herbert service by ringing your local Distribution Centre. Anytime.

Figure 12. Herbert Tooling "phone-in" example.

number of automatic dialing systems which can be installed to make it possible for your sales people to reach the people they must contact with greater ease and speed. If you get in touch with the people in your local telephone company business office, they will be able to inform you what systems are available in your area.

When the tele-sales system has been working smoothly and successfully for a year or so, you may like to get it doing a little more—like handling a few *difficult* customers with whom the salesmen cannot get on.

Firms like Birds Eye, Ross Foods, and Coca-Cola in the consumer sales side of the business now generate more than 80 percent of their total sales through tele-sales operations.

Ross Foods has calculated that the total cost of a tele-sales call is one-third the cost of a face-to-face call by a salesman. The average length of a Ross tele-sales call is 3.7 minutes, compared with the average length of a face-to-face call of 20 minutes.

Average cost of a tele-sales call (total costs) working on an area of 50-mile maximum radius from base, and calculated on telephone charge rates, is about $3 per call.

Here is an example of a job specification for a Tele-Sales Operator at Ross Foods. From this you will see the kind of sophisticated activities the operators are expected to perform—and which they do, very successfully.

JOB SPECIFICATION FOR A TELE-SALES OPERATOR

Job Title: Tele-Sales Operator
Department: Sales
Responsible to: District Manager
Works in Close Association with: All plant and warehouse management, respresentatives, and distribution managers.

Main Purposes and Scope of the Job: To service via the telephone a predetermined number of calls and, in doing so, to promote the sale of the company's products to reach the targets and objectives set.

Responsibilities and Duties:

1. It is the tele-sales operator's responsibility to see that every one of his or her customers is contacted on the day prescribed in the customer file according to the call rate set.

2. As the job is based on a sales and service principle, the tele-sales operator is expected to use his or her skills to ensure that adequate stocks are held of those products and packages purchased by the customer to last between each telephone call.

3. To inform the customer at every opportunity of the products and services available from the company and, in doing so, endeavor to improve on the product and pack holding and volume throughout.

4. To optimize on all sales promotions when run.

5. To work in close liaison with the sales representatives with a view to improving the management and development of their area.

6. To keep management informed at all times of dealer wants and needs. Furthermore to follow up on all competitive activity.

7. To receive and act upon telephone orders that come into the plant or depot and to control the buying stability of outlets under his or her control.

8. To ensure that all documents are legible and correctly filled out.

9. To keep adequate records of daily activity such as calls made, buyers, nonbuyers, and sales by pack and product, including new packs or products introduced, so that the daily, weekly, and monthly reports can be raised.

10. To ensure that all dealer record cards are updated at all times.

11. To attend sales training meetings or conferences held by local management or by the company.

In his or her capacity as a tele-sales operator, the employee will be responsible to management for:

A quantifiable number of route customer calls
Telephone-sales communications with the trade
Customer relations within the work section
Personal selling to existing customers
Sales development of route calls
Clerical processing of relevant administration
Statistical control of sales targets and performance
The recording and reporting of all relevant information and
    sales data

Route calls—as required by management to provide full cover of a normal working day in relation to specific targets.

Telephone communications—by establishing verbal communications on a regular and planned basis, with clarity, manner, knowledge, and personality.

Customer relations—by establishing goodwill and credibility between the customer, the tele-sales operator, and the company by service, reliability, and helping to solve dealer problems.

Personal selling—by direct telephone selling, with the buyer, on all existing accounts.

Sales development—by personal planning from information recorded on the sales record cards. Maximize sales using the full range of products and packages available, by knowledgeable presentation allied to any promotional activities currently operating with the trade.

Clerical processing—by accurate utilization of all relevant documentation associated with customer orders and allied paperwork.

Statistical control—by regular attention to set targets and performance figures as laid down by management.

Recording—by regular utilization of all relevant documentation in line with tele-sales operator's activities and duties on all aspects of control procedures associated with his or her employment.

Reporting—by the operator's regular submission of all relevant information in reference to the work and the customers, together with any problem associated.

Memos to the Troops

Anything in writing is highly dangerous, because words can be interpreted in so many different ways. Few managers ever bother about this. Worse still, many managers never sent memos to their troops at all.

Regular communication between manager and salesmen is essential. Out there in the field, it's a lonely job. A salesman needs to feel wanted, to be told often that he is doing a good job. It's part of motivation.

Memos come in all shapes and sizes. The simplest and most effective in motivational terms are the "well done" kind.

Just a note to say, "well done" on the Radford order, George. Their purchasing people are a bunch of hard nuts to crack. Keep up the good work!

This will be doubly effective, because invariably the salesman's wife will read it.

Memos that bring *change* are the most dangerous kind— change in procedures, change of policy, change of prices, change in delivery schedules.

The secret for these kind of memos is always to explain *why* the change is necessary, and then to go on and explain the benefits to the company, the salesmen, or whatever, that will result from the change—*in simple language.*

Now dig out a few of the memos you have sent out to your troops over the past weeks, and have a good nightmare.

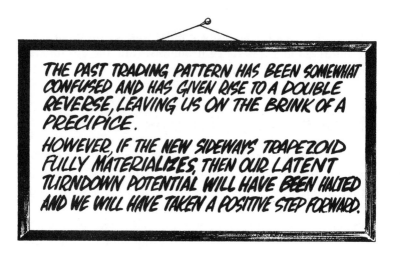

Moonlighting

Moonlighters are harder to catch than con artists. Either they use their energies in pursuing another after-hours job, or, worse still, they sell someone else's products at the same time as they are selling yours, and to the same customers.

Do not ever advocate, encourage, or allow any form of moonlighting. If a salesman isn't totally committed to your company, its objectives, and his target, get rid of him.

I've known salesmen with their own businesses with dress shops, which they run on Saturdays; with fish and chip saloons; with market stalls; who act as barmen every night of the week; who play in dance bands; who sell insurance on the side; who are part-time lecturers at technical colleges; who trade in antiques, jewelry, porn, contraceptives, instant print; and who sell advertising space as well as forklift trucks. Any kind of moonlighting saps your employee's energies and *you* lose. Make sure all your salesman are prohibited from carrying on any other kind of business activity by building an appropriate clause into their service contracts.

If you have such a clause, and you catch someone moonlighting, fire him on the spot. And make sure the rest of the team knows why.

According to the Bureau of Labor Statistics, there were 4.5 million known moonlighters in the United States in 1978. Because many Americans take second jobs "off the books," however, the actual number is probably a good deal higher.

Motivation

For any kind of motivation to work, it has to relate to something that will happen in the *future*—not the present or the past.

Thus, it is no use paying a salesman more money in the hope that he will perform better in the months ahead. He won't, and you'll never be able to take the extra money back from him, either. A month after its award, he'll firmly believe he got it by right.

There are two kinds of motivation, negative and positive. Negative is commonly referred to as the "Big Stick," and uses fear as its main weapon. Positive is commonly referred to as the "Carrot," and uses pleasurable or better things to look forward to as its main tool.

The Big Stick doesn't work anymore, except with salesmen of elderly years, who know they won't get another job if they lose the one they have. With younger salesmen, they'll take only so much, then they'll tell you what to do with the job and leave of their own accord. Motivating by fear is both futile and senseless.

For the Carrot to work in making salesmen strive for greater things, the Carrot itself must be seen by all to be attainable. If it is too far out of reach, only the high flyers will make any effort to reach it; the rest will quickly decide there is no point in trying.

Motivation is like the weather—constantly changing. What turns one man on one year may not turn him on the next. Always be aware of this. Keep up to date. And remember, everyone is different. What motivates one salesman may not work on the others. Tailor your motivational package to each individual.

Norms

In the section, "Personal Performance," I discuss a system for measuring and monitoring each salesman's effectiveness.

If you take the quarterly totals for each of your salesmen and add them together, you can calculate performance norms for the sales force as a whole.

Figures 13 and 14 show examples of how to produce Norms and sales force totals on just two pieces of specially designed card.

The value in calculating Norms for performance is:

1. Each salesman can relate his own performance, in detail, to the average (Norm) performance for the sales force as a whole.

2. Where any salesman has a personal performance ratio worse than the Norm ratio, he strives during the next quarter to bring his performance at least up to the Norm performance.

3. In achieving this improvement, the company Norms for the next quarter are automatically better than for the last quarter.

4. The whole process then becomes *automatic*. Performance steadily improves because no one wants a ratio worse than the Norm. You can almost sit back and let it happen.

Office Costs

One of your objectives is to keep them as low as possible, just like salesmen's expenses.

Get all your office staff to work at the checklist shown in Figure 15. It doesn't just aim itself at reducing costs; it is also useful for improving office efficiency.

Organizing Sales Conferences

Most companies hold an annual sales conference. The conference usually analyzes the performance of the last sales period and then goes into plans for the next sales period. Individual members of the company get up and talk about various specific subjects and a couple of visiting speakers may be

REF MR 1

COMPANY NORMS							PERIOD	SECOND QUARTER WEEKS 14 TO 26		
SALESMAN	TOTAL CALLS	NO INTER-VIEWS	CALLS ON USERS	ORDERS FROM USERS	TOTAL ORDER VALUE FROM USERS	FIRST EVER CALLS	CALLS ON PROSP'TS	PROP'LS SUBM-ITTED	ORDERS FROM PROSP'TS	TOTAL ORDER VALUE FROM PROSPECTS
1 J. WATSON	288	44	203	44	13,884	46	85	23	18	4,669
2 R. BRIGGS	264	32	168	27	8,963	51	96	44	27	6,463
3 L. SUTTON	249	28	202	31	9,275	36	47	11	8	2,761
4 F. VINTERS	296	31	175	27	8,740	68	121	57	31	7,892
5 G. HOPKINS	721	43	212	41	8,202	59	109	49	28	6,720
6 A. ROLFE	199	37	142	20	7,966	29	57	19	14	7,995
7 B. STEIN	255	42	170	26	8,449	56	85	39	22	5,977
8 S. ARMSTRONG	253	30	166	32	9,791	66	87	48	24	6,502
9 J. TONES	241	21	175	31	9,464	41	66	35	20	4,744
10 W. ASQUITH	702	26	204	52	13,242	64	98	52	29	8,842
11										
12										
13										
14										
15										
16										
17										
18										
19										
20										
21										
22										
23										
24										
25										
TOTALS	2,668	334	1,817	331	97,976	516	851	387	221	58,565
	A	B	C	D	E	F	G	H	J	K

SALES CONTROL & RECORD SYSTEMS LTD

Abortive call Ratio $\dfrac{A\ 2668}{B\ 334} = \boxed{8.0 \text{ to} 1}$

Average calls on a Prospect $\dfrac{G\ 851}{F\ 516} = \boxed{1.65}$

Calls to proposals Ratio (Prospects) $\dfrac{G\ 851}{H\ 387} = \boxed{2.2 \text{ to} 1}$

Calls to orders Ratio (Users) $\dfrac{C\ 1817}{D\ 331} = \boxed{5.5 \text{ to} 1}$

Proposals to orders Ratio (Prospects) $\dfrac{H\ 387}{J\ 221} = \boxed{1.75 \text{ to} 1}$

Average order Value (Users) $\dfrac{E\ 97976}{D\ 331} = \boxed{\$296}$

Average order Value (Prospects) $\dfrac{K\ 58565}{J\ 221} = \boxed{\$265}$

Figure 13. Company norms card.

© SALES CONTROL & RECORD SYSTEMS LTD.

REF MR 2

ACTIVITY ANALYSIS

PERIOD ____

SALESMAN			
1. WATSON			
2. R. BURGESS			
3. L. SUTTON			
4. F. WINTERS			
5. G. HOPKINS			
6. A. ROLFE			
7. D. STEIN			
8. S. ARMSTRONG			
9. J. TONER			
11 W. ARGYLL			

TOTALS

Figure 14. Activity analysis card.

	N/A	YES	NO	PAR	?	ACT
1. Do all departments conform to a uniform filing system?						
2. If no, does this lead to confusion when staff are 'on loan' from another department?						
3. . . . . or to any other form of delay or confusion?						
4. Is our present system simple enough to enable junior staff to rapidly retrieve files and documents?						
5. Are our filing procedures formalized and in writing for the benefit of new management and staff?						
6. Do we have over-duplication of information (copies or documents which are filed and never again referred to)?						
7. Do we have under-duplication of information (constant requests between departments for files and documents)?						
8. Do we have rigid accountability on all photocopying?						
9. . . . . and do we occasionally check that copies in excess of requirements are not being produced?						
10. Are telephone switchboard procedures in writing?						
11. Do we fully appreciate the importance of efficient switchboard operation?						
12. . . . . and the need to maintain this particular 'Company image' at the highest possible level?						
13. Is the switchboard operator advised daily about those Executives who are away?						
14. . . . . and also advised of those who will be absent for several hours?						
15. Do secretaries/typists frequently await incoming mail to be processed before they can commence work?						
16. Does the sorting and distribution of mail receive priority every morning?						
17. . . . . and subsequent mail likewise?						
18. If no, does this result in operational delays and/or executives and their secretaries working overtime in order to process the mail?						
19. Do any executives/managers have semi-idle secretaries because they regularly delay processing their correspondence?						
20. If yes, could staff reductions be made if they processed more promptly?						
21. . . . . or conversely, could staff be made available to them in the latter part of the day, and thus reduce staff?						
22. . . . . or if dictation equipment were to be installed?						
23. Have we assessed the level of activity at which we should review/introduce dictation equipment?						
24. If it became necessary, for financial reasons, for staff to be reduced by 20%, do we know *now* how these reductions would be effected?						
25. Could any such reductions be made now—without serious loss of efficiency?						
26. If yes, have we prepared recommendations to this effect and submitted them to senior management?						
27. Are workloads reasonably and evenly distributed among female staff?						
28. In order to minimize typing have we analyzed our correspondence within the last 12 months with a view to standardization of replies that are in common and repetitive use?						
29. Have our present standard letters been reviewed within the last 12 months?						

Figure 15.   Office activity checklist.

brought in from outside to give a fresh approach to some sales point or another.

Or the company may run an annual sales training session and use its own management to do the actual training, if it is capable. Either way, two or three days are involved, and the entire sales force has to be accommodated around the venue for the duration of the festivities.

There are several important factors that contribute to a successful conference. The first is to gain the maximum amount of participation from *all* the people there. Without this, the ultimate objective will never be attained—that everyone should go away from the conference totally committed to the plans discussed and firmly believing that they are right.

Conferences should not be used as an opportunity for management to lean heavily on the sales force, and any form of oppression should be avoided. Oppression can come in various forms. Enclosed by just the four walls of his head office, a salesman can feel intimidated by his surroundings, switch to the defensive, and shut up like a clam for the entire proceedings. This varies with the company, of course, but the first general rule for running conferences is:

Avoid Having Them on Company Premises

Apart from the reason just expounded, few companies have the right facilities for a successful conference. The time wasted shuttling back and forth for meals at a nearby hotel and sorting out accommodations in similar adjacent abodes, usually costs as much as if the company had put the entire thing into the right sort of hotel in the first place. Which brings us to our second general rule:

Select the Right Sort of Hotel

Of course, cost is an important factor, but the cost difference between a good and a bad hotel is insignificant when compared with the value of increased business which the

company wants the conference to launch. A bad hotel can
ruin a whole year's motivation and performance.
The right sort of hotel should have the following facilities:

1. Single bedrooms with their own bathrooms. (Make the
   sales force look forward to the event.)
2. A really good restaurant. (Remember, the way to a man's
   heart is through his stomach—it's true for salesmen, too.)
3. Really comfortable chairs in the conference room. (The
   mind can only absorb as much as the behind can en-
   dure.)
4. The right shaped conference room—and large enough,
   with plenty of air. If in doubt, always double the size.
   More about the right shape later, under "Get the Room
   Layout Right."
5. Good visual aids. (That means blackboards, flipcharts,
   movie screens, projectors, ways of effectively blacking
   out the room during film showings, good lighting and
   microphones for speakers, and so forth.)
6. A staff that knows about the conference business. (Nothing can break a conference organizer's heart quicker than
   having a hotel staff that hasn't a clue about what a good
   conference needs.)
7. Adequate car parking.
8. Silence. (Never pick a hotel on a main highway, or in the
   center of a town. If in doubt, stay for a night yourself and
   see.)

One point when booking reservations for a conference—never
rely on the telephone alone. Go and see for yourself. I only
made this mistake once, in London. Never again will I rely on
a hotel manager's verbal interpretation. It wasn't really the
manager's fault; I failed to convey to him what I was looking
for. It's so easily done, especially when time is short.
And so to the third general rule:

Get the Room Layout Right

I know a hotel that has recently spent nearly $250,000 on a new conference wing. I will never use it. Whoever designed the new wing obviously had no idea of how a good conference should be run. The "sharp end" of the room, where the speaker has to stand, has superb picture windows. Did you ever try to concentrate on a speaker on a summer afternoon when he's standing in front of dazzling sunlight? The strain is tremendous. The audience cannot see a thing. Again, the entrances to the conference room are close to the picture windows. So anyone creeping in and out can be seen by the entire audience. Another concentration sapper. It may sound petty to you, but it really is very important.

For a really effective conference—or training session—the audience should face a blank wall. Windows should preferably be behind the audience, so that the delegates cannot even glance out every time a pretty girl passes by. The only objects in front of that blank wall should be the visual aids being used: the blackboard, the flipchart, the movie screen. Entrances should always, but *always*, be at the back of the room. As conference organizer yourself, you will be in and out all the time, sorting out minor details.

Always provide your delegates with tables. I have seen so many conferences where the delegates sat theater style for three whole days with nowhere to write notes, nowhere to lean elbows and ease the aching behind. Disaster. The optimal layout of tables and chairs is as shown in the diagram, Figure 16. Nobody in the room has to angle his head or body more than 15 degrees either way to see everything going on at the front.

The square layout shown in Figure 17 is sometimes preferred. It is satisfactory for a group discussion, where everyone around the square is participating, but if there are speakers using one end (especially ones who like walking a lot, as I do), it takes only half an hour for some of the delegates to get cricks in their necks.

Allow at least three feet of table per person, and make sure there is always adequate fresh water available for all.

Now a few words about the format of the actual conference itself. Try to split the entire proceedings into sessions of not more than one hour duration. Use films between formal sessions so that the whole day's work is as diverse as possible. If the day starts at 9:00 A.M., have a coffee break at about 10:00

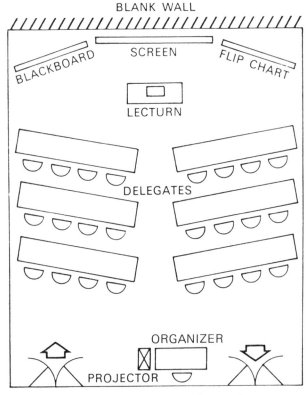

Figure 16. Optimum conference layout.

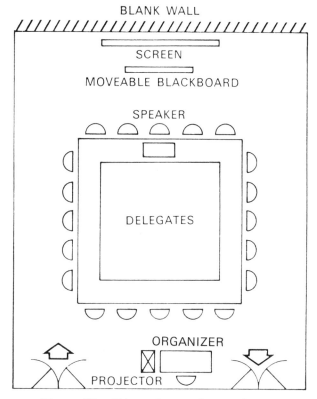

Figure 17. Discussion conference layout.

A.M. and lunch at about 12:00 P.M. Another coffee break at about 3:00 P.M. then leaves only two hours before normal finishing time.

If your company prefers to use the evenings as well (a sentiment with which I heartily concur), break for dinner early and then go back afterward. But try not to have any really heavy stuff for the after-dinner business. The levels of concentration will be only half what they were in the morning.

As organizer, it is your job to make sure the drinking water is changed at each break, 9:00 A.M., 11:00 A.M., 12:00 noon, and 3:00 P.M. A good hotel staff will automatically do this, but do not rely on them for the first day, just in case. Try to take coffee and tea in another room, so that everyone can stretch his legs. After lunch, insist that each delegate take a walk around the hotel to get some fresh air. It makes all the difference to the number of yawns during the afternoon.

Keep to the Timetable

Don't allow anyone to run over his allotted time—even the president! If you do, the whole proceedings can quickly come down around your ears. And while we are talking about the timetable, and your months of planning before the actual conference—because that's how long it takes—remember that most good hotels are taking bookings up to *two years* in advance, so don't leave everything until the last minute. Films need advance booking notice to make absolutely sure of getting them on the right day.

REGIONAL SALES MEETINGS

Many companies have regional managers whose job it is to train and motivate the salesmen under their command. To do this, regional managers hold meetings once a month, or once a quarter.

The same rules we have discussed for sales conferences also apply to these smaller meetings—except, of course, that there is no accommodation requirement. But a professional outlook on such a meeting by the regional manager can work wonders in motivation. I've also seen exactly the opposite—a half-day affair in a shabby little room with no heating—which had such a demoralizing effect on the salesmen that the regional manager was openly held in derision by his men.

Personal Performance

Most sales managers would say that measuring and monitoring a salesman's performance or effectiveness is one of the most difficult and elusive things to get your teeth into. Not so. It's the way they try to measure and monitor which makes the job difficult. Done properly, monitoring personal performance is one of the easiest jobs the sales manager has to do, and one of the least time-consuming.

I've spent about ten years developing systems for sales force control, and in this section I'm going to discuss what I consider is the best—S.C.R.S., marketed by Sales Control and Record Systems Ltd. Other parts of the S.C.R.S. system are mentioned in the sections entitled "Norms," "Forecasting," "Customer Records," and "If in Doubt—Ask."

BASIC PRINCIPLE

A sales force control measuring or monitoring system *must* use numbers, *not* words.

All you can do with words is read them. You can't add them up, multiply them, divide them, or anything. So all you get with words is an instant picture of today or yesterday. No sales manager has a computer for a mind, so he cannot correlate all the words he receives from his salesmen and put together an ongoing picture. He'd go mad if he tried.

You cannot judge the performance of a salesman solely on the turnover he produces in a given period of time, or on the number of calls he makes each week. Personal performance measurement needs to cover much more. Here's the most effective way of doing the job properly.

Each week, every salesman submits to you a list of *all* the face-to-face calls he has made during the week, and what happened on each call. This list does *not* include telephone calls. This weekly list is in the form shown in Figure 18 and is

DATE	COMPANY	Industry Category	No Interview	Call on Existing Customer	Call on Prospect (Pot. New Cust.)	First Ever Call	Follow up of Lead	Appointment	Proposal Requested	Action Request	Order Secured	Service Call	0	1	2	3	4	5	6	7	8	9
M	PRESS STEEL	A	✓					✓														✓
"	POTTERSBY & Co.	B	✓		✓	✓								✓								
"	J & B ENGINEERS	A		✓																		✓	
"	HEREFORD & Co.	D		✓				✓		✓	✓											✓	
"	EATON & Co	C		✓												✓	✓						
T	WYMAN WELDING	B		✓											✓							
"	I.B.E.	D		✓	✓																	✓
"	SMITH DAVIDSON	B	✓		✓	✓																
"	FISHER & WADE	D		✓			✓	✓	✓	✓										✓			
"	AUTOLIFT	B		✓															✓				✓
"	VICTORIA FORGE	A		✓	✓																	✓	
"	ASH & Co	A	✓	✓																		
"	BLOGGS & SMALL	A		✓																✓	✓		✓
"	EXHALL TOOLS	D		✓				✓															✓
W	JONES & PLATT	B		✓			✓		✓	✓										✓			
"	BREEDON SMITH	G		✓													✓	✓					
"	DROP FORGES	A		✓			✓		✓	✓												✓
"	F. LACEY & Co.	B			✓		✓	✓														✓
-	ARUNDEL DEVEL.	G			✓	✓			✓	✓										✓			
F	CK VALVES	D	✓	✓																		
"	BRITISH STEEL	A		✓				✓														✓	
"	AQUASCUTUM	K			✓			✓		✓											✓		
"	BR. SEALED BEAMS	J		✓			✓	✓	✓	✓										✓			
"	WAKEFIELDS	C		✓																	✓		
"	APPLEGATE & G.	A		✓																✓			
"	GOLDEN WONDER	K		✓				✓		✓	✓									✓			
	TOTALS		4	18	8	5	3	11	3	7	5	0	2	1	4	5	1	0	3	2	7	2

Product Groups Discussed totals: 0 1 2 3 4 5 6 7 8 9

	0	1	2	3	4	5	6	7	8	9
	2	1	4	5	1	0	3	2	7	2

NUMBER OF PROPOSALS SUBMITTED ON PROSPECTS (POT. NEW CUSTOMERS) DURING WEEK: **2**

	A	B	C	D	E	F	G	H	J	K
INDUSTRY CATEGORY TOTALS	8	6	2	5	0	0	2	0	1	2

BUSINESS MILEAGE: **245**

IF A CALL RESULTS IN "NO INTERVIEW" STILL TICK THE COLUMNS WHICH INDICATE WHAT KIND OF CALL IT SHOULD HAVE BEEN.

Figure 18. Call analysis form.

entitled "Call Analysis." The design of the form reduces writing to a minimum. Each call takes up one line, most of the "what happened" data being recorded as ticks. The sections covering "Industry Category" and "Product Groups Discussed" use a master code devised by the company and common to all the salesmen. Our example shows the calls salesman J. Watson made during week 14 of the year in question. He traveled 245 miles to make the calls, and (bottom left) succeeded in submitting 2 proposals on prospects (not to be confused with existing customers) during the week.

You will receive one of these forms from each of your salesmen in each Monday's mail along with expense claims and call plans for the next week. All you do with the information is enter the totals on two master cards you keep for each salesman. The work of entering the totals on these cards each Monday takes a few minutes only. In fact, your secretary should do it.

Figures 19 and 20 show the two master cards for salesman J. Watson. Following the numbers through from our example of his week 14 Call Analysis form, you will see that the totals are entered in the week 14 lines on these two cards.

Four items of information must be supplied each week from headquarters (usually Accounts) to complete each salesman's cards. These items are the total orders received from existing customers during the week from each salesman's territory and the total value of these orders and likewise for prospects.

The two master cards are designed to calculate performance on a quarterly basis, which has been found to be by far the most suitable period, being long enough to iron out any abnormalities in the numbers due to holidays or illness and short enough to give the company time to sort out any major problems the numbers pinpoint before these problems get out of hand.

Apart from entering the numbers on these cards each Monday, there is no further action necessary until the end of

Figure 19. Personal performance record card.

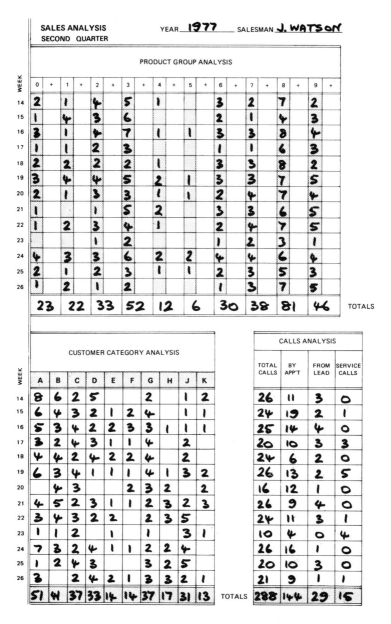

Figure 20. Sales analysis card.

the 13-week period—in our case, after the end of week 26. Then you or your secretary total all the columns and by dividing the smaller totals into the larger for each pair of numbers on the Personal Performance Record card (Figure 19), you calculate each salesman's performance for that quarter with respect to *eight* different aspects of his job.

From the totals on the Sales Analysis master card (Figure 20), you pinpoint any part of the product range that a salesman might be neglecting, and likewise for any industry important to the company. The bottom right column totals give you information on how effective each salesman is at making appointments, how effective your sales promotion and advertising activities have been in each territory, and how much time each salesman has been forced to spend on non-selling activities.

This is all the data you need, on two A4-size cards, to pinpoint specific problems and implement remedial action without delay.

By comparing one quarter's figures with another's, a pattern of personal performance can clearly be established. The ratios are also extremely valuable in calculating accurate and attainable sales targets for each salesman, but this we have discussed under "Forecasting."

To find out what else can be done with these cards, read the section on "Norms."

Post-Mortems

Always find out in detail why an important piece of business the company was chasing was lost. Get everyone together and hold a post-mortem. You need to pinpoint all the reasons you lost the order, so that everyone can make sure the same mistakes don't get made again.

But make sure your post-mortems don't develop into

hatchet meetings or recrimination sessions. If they do, you'll never find out what went wrong.

Priorities

Always get your priorities in the right order.

Start each week by getting together with your secretary and listing the things that *must* be done that week. Then list the things that *should* be done. Then list the things that *could* be done, given the time.

Never get your *musts*, *shoulds*, and *coulds* mixed up. And always make sure everyone in your department knows what's on the list (except for any confidential matters, of course). This way, your staff will *help* you complete the list, rather than hinder you.

Figure 21 shows an example of a daily job-priority form, used for sales promotional purposes by a printing group.

Musts for Today

Date

URGENT   DONE
☐ _____ ☐
☐ _____ ☐
☐ _____ ☐
☐ _____ ☐
☐ _____ ☐
☐ _____ ☐
☐ _____ ☐
☐ _____ ☐
☐ _____ ☐
☐ _____ ☐
☐ _____ ☐
☐ _____ ☐
☐ _____ ☐
☐ _____ ☐
☐ _____ ☐
☐ _____ ☐
☐ _____ ☐
☐ _____ ☐
☐ _____ ☐
☐ _____ ☐
☐ _____ ☐
☐ _____ ☐
☐ _____ ☐
☐ _____ ☐
☐ _____ ☐
☑ *Phone Headquarters* _____ ☐

Figure 21.   Daily job-priority form ("Musts for Today").

Quotations and Proposals

Only if you are selling at the lowest price and with the shortest delivery will you get away with using the traditional legal quotation, full of Victoriana (thank you for your esteemed . . .), technical specification, terms of payment, price, and with all the terms and conditions for doing business in pale gray 6 pt. type on the back.

If you haven't got the lowest price or the shortest delivery, you will be losing most of the business that you quote for. Change the rules. Change the way you quote and start submitting decent selling proposals.

I cannot do better, in explaining how and why, than to reproduce an article I wrote recently for the Institute of Purchasing Management.

DON'T ACCEPT THE LOWEST BID

From time to time, every buyer has to suffer from the traditional task of collecting quotations from selected suppliers for a particular requirement and, having received the quotations, trying to analyze the gobbledygook and to decide which of the offers gives him the best all-around deal.

No longer is price the only consideration, of course. Quality, performance, maintenance costs, delivery, and reliability are all factors which will influence the final decision one way or the other.

But it does often seem to be far too difficult for the buyer to establish which of, say, three or four quotations is really the best bet. Suppliers are loath to submit quotations with information that is going to make the job easier.

Here's a good example:

Dear Sirs,

We beg to thank you for your esteemed enquiry, and have pleasure in quoting as follows, subject to the terms and conditions stated on the back hereof:

Four lanes of Bloggs Proximity Dual Duty Overhead Conveyors Kx 500/4.

Loading 1200 lb per trolley.

Speed 60 feet per minute.

Automatic electronic beam safety equipment fitted every 20 foot run.

All basically in accordance with customer drawing 2B/42/764.

For the sum of $d4,764.50.

Delivery 18–22 weeks from confirmation of official customer order.

Terms of payment: Net cash 30 days.

Prices hold good for 60 days only from date of this quotation.

We trust that the above quotation will prove to be satisfactory, and we look forward to the receipt of your esteemed order in due course, when it will receive our most careful attention.

Yours faithfully,

Per Pro Bloggs Handling Inc.

Every time I see a quotation like that, it makes me sigh heavily and gives me indigestion for a week. Do suppliers honestly think they can still get business with this kind of drivel? Do they ever stop to think what the poor old buyer is up against on the receiving end?

Specification–Price–Delivery. Just that and nothing more. Specification–Price–Delivery. Not even any attempt to ex-

plain what the hell a Bloggs Proximity Dual Duty Overhead
Conveyor is—or what it does. Okay, the salesman told you a
month ago, and the leaflet is lying around somewhere, but do
they really expect you to remember all that technical jargon
the salesman exlained to you four or five weeks back? If they
do, they're nuts! What proportion of your total time has this
job they're quoting for taken up these last four weeks: 5 percent? 2 percent? Let's see them remember much of a discussion a month ago when 98 percent of their time has been taken
up with other problems and requirements, most of them just
as important, or more so.

So there is the buyer, sitting at his desk, looking at three
or four typical quotations. Specification–Price–Delivery.
Specification–Price–Delivery. Hey, this one doesn't even give
a spec. It's just a list of equipment with prices, totaled at the
bottom.

Which offer does he decide to accept?

If we assume that Delivery is not a critical factor in the
particular case we are examining, or alternatively, that all the
quotations offer an acceptable delivery, the entire decision-
making exercise hangs on the specification and the price.

So specifications are examined closely. The snag is, there is
so little meaningful information. All the buyer (or his engineer) can do is establish whether or not the equipment offered will meet the criteria laid down—whether it will, in fact,
do the job the company wants done. Not how *well* it will do
the job. Not how much *better* it will do the job than the criteria
laid down. Not how it will do the job in a different and more
efficient way than the company stipulated.

Just that it will do the job that has to be done. A minimum
specification requirement if you like.

There is our poor buyer, faced with three or four pos-
sibilities, all of which will satisfy the minimum requirements,
but none of which tell him how much *better* they are. Whether

they qualify for a "credit" or a "distinction," rather than a pass.

So, like many an examiner in academic circles, our buyer wields his rubber stamp *pass* on all the quotations. Delivery dealt with. Specification dealt with.

That leaves only price—and faced with this particular set of circumstances, only a fool would order anything but the cheapest. The quotation offering the lowest price *should* get the order, and most of the time does.

But has the buyer made sure his company has the best deal? I say *no*.

Not his fault entirely. To make absolutely sure, he needs to examine very closely indeed each piece of equipment offered, to compare specifications, and to translate the specifications into figures or facts meaningful to him and his company's requirement. Then he must project those facts and figures over a period of time to establish overall gains, savings, maintenance costs, etc.; and to allow for labor, cost of finance, sales forecasts for established production, and so on, in order to arrive at a true comparison of offer to offer.

Only then can he turn to price and decide which one to buy. And only then will he be able to use his comparison calculations to prove that, despite a price $1,000 higher than the offer from A, offer B gives a better overall deal, and the extra price paid will be recouped in maintenance savings, less scrap, higher output, reduced labor, etc., within the first six months.

So B gets the order. But can the buyer really be expected to go to all that trouble? Shouldn't it be the supplier's job to demonstrate how good the equipment offered is for the buyer's company?

If *you* think, as I do, that providing this all-important information is the supplier's job, here is a plan for getting *your* future suppliers to do *their* job properly, and thus save you a whole lot of effort and grief.

In a very much simplified form, give the suppliers some clear-cut instructions on how to tender for your business. Not

specially laid out tender forms, as local authorities use, but just a single sheet of instructions. For example:

To: All Suppliers
From: J. E. Fenton, Chief Buyer
Subject: Procedure for submitting quotations

All quotations to this company should give the information as below and in the chronological order shown below. Quotations which do not follow this procedure will not be considered.

1. Begin all quotations with a brief statement of the objectives we wish to achieve by having your equipment/products/services.

2. Follow this statement of objectives with a brief outline of your recommendations, and explain—briefly—how your recommendations fulfill our objectives.

3. Elaborate on item 2 with a list of any additional benefits we will receive from your recommendations, other than the information given under item 2.

4. Explain, with the full use of figures, finance, times, labor rates, maintenance costs, depreciation periods, production outputs—whichever are relevant—how we can justify the purchase of the equipment/products/services. All prices must be inclusive—that is, they must include delivery, installation, commissioning, or whatever else is necessary.

5. State the guarantee you provide, give details of your after-sales service organization and how it operates, and add at least three third-party references that we can contact, i.e., firms using similar equipment/products/services and in our area.

Finally, don't write your quotations in stiff, formal prose (for example, "thank you for your esteemed enquiry," "look forward to the favor of," etc.); write it in plain, modern English.

The result of such a set of instructions could be something like this.

Remember the Bloggs Proximity Dual Duty Overhead Conveyor? Well, the opening section of the "new look" quotation might now read:

"As we understand it, you require:
- A fully automatic means of transporting up to 600 car bodies an hour across the roads which separate your No. 1 and No. 2 assembly shops.
- A built-in safety system which will instantly stop the above transportation in the event of the body units becoming dislodged.
- Installation of the system so as to cause minimum disruption of your production flow.

Quite a bit more meaningful, don't you think?

Here's another example of opening objectives.

We agreed at our last discussion that you wanted to achieve the following:
- Provide mechanized handling facilities to enable up to 2,000 tons of fragile cargo to be off-loaded from ship to shore during one normal working shift.
- Extend these facilities by the end of the first year's operation so as to completely turn around a 10,000–15,000 ton cargo vessel in 36 hours.
- Provide full training for your staff in the operation and maintenance of the equipment needed for these facilities.

These kinds of opening sections set the scene for the rest of the quotation.

The most important section for any buyer in this new style of quotation is *Financial Justification*. This is the information which really makes it easy for you to compare a number of

offers and to pinpoint the best. This is where the supplier tells you what you are getting for your money.

Example 1
Your existing handling plant effects an output of 100 units per hour, on a 24-hour basis.

The proposed new system will increase this output to 150 units per hour.

This gives you an increase in production, in terms of output, of 3,600 units per day, or 1,315,000 units per year, or 6,560,000 units in the five-year period over which you would write off the plant's depreciation.

Example 2
If you install this equipment, the labor force necessary for the handling operations can be reduced by four people.

Estimating a warehouseman's costs to your company at $200 per week, this would represent a saving on labor costs alone of $800 per week or $38,400 in the first year.

On an initial capital investment of $14,764.50, the cost will be recovered from these labor savings in

$$\frac{14,764.50}{38,400} = 0.384 \text{ years, or } 4.6 \text{ months}$$

Over your normal five-year depreciation period for this type of plant, and assuming a labor cost increase of 10 percent per year, your net savings would be as follows:

1st year labor saving	$ 38,400
2nd year labor saving	42,240
3rd year labor saving	46,464
4th year labor saving	51,110
5th year labor saving	56,221
	$234,435
less cost of equipment	14,764.50
Net Saving	$219,670.50

(I am tempted to add at this point that if you have the task of justifying any purchase of capital equipment to your own board of directors, these are the kind of figures that will make that job very easy. And if those pessimists at the top *still* say the company can't afford it, there is another arrow still to be fired.)

Example 3

If you were to lease this equipment over five years, the cost of the rentals each week, on a capital price of $14,764.50, would be $75.67 per week.

Your labor savings amount to $800 per week in the first year, more in subsequent years. Thus, if you lease the equipment, it won't cost one penny and will save you upwards of $720 per week.

Example 4

Financial justification can be set out for products like pumps, valves, fluorescent lightfittings, electronic components, and a host more, as well as for production equipment.

Let's take a ball valve. A particularly fine valve. Better than anything else on the market. For one specific size, the cost of the valve is $40.

But when this ball valve was introduced, the market had been buying ball valves for $10 to do the jobs this new valve was designed to do.

Imagine the reception given by any buyer to a Specification–Price–Delivery quotation for this new valve.

"Four times the price? You must be joking!"

So back to the financial justification. The key benefit of the new valve was its lack of the need for maintenance. Packings had to be replaced only once a year, and even then, could be done very quickly. The old $10 valves lasted only two months before the packings needed replacement, and it was such a messy job that the plant engineers usually threw the whole valve away and installed a new one.

On this basis, the following comparison costing was put together by the $40 valve suppliers:

MAINTENANCE COSTS PER YEAR PER VALVE

	New Valve	Old Valve
Initial cost of valve	$40	$10
Packing replacements required	1	6
Time allowed for replacement	20 minutes	2 hours
Therefore Total replacement time/ year	20 minutes	12 hours
Packing costs	$1	—
Replacement valve costs	—	$60 (6 × $10)
Plant engineers' labor costs based on $30 per hour incl. overheads	$10	$360
Total costs per year per valve	$51	$430

Note: These calculations do not attempt to calculate the cost of 12 hours production per year while the valves are being replaced. This cost should be added to the $430, and likewise, the cost of 20 minutes lost production should be added to the $51.

See how much more effective those quotations could be? And how much easier it would be for you to make the *right* decision every time.

Draft a set of quotation instructions for your own business. Insist on suppliers adhering to them. Try it out on just a few for a start if you like. It's the best way of avoiding that trap we started with—being tempted to accept the lowest bid.

If your salesmen are selling lumps of machinery or any other kind of capital equipment, there is much more that they can, and should, do to back up the Financial Justification for the purchase in their proposals.

Recruiting Salesmen

Whether you recruit a clerk or a chief executive, the worldwide average for employees recruited who are acceptable and successful in their new job after one year is only 50 percent.

So don't go overboard on sophisticated psychological recruitment techniques or personal recriminations. Here are a few rules to follow when recruiting salesmen:

1. Be very hard-nosed about anyone who is willing to move to you for the same or less money than he was getting in his last selling job. Face facts: he's an idiot, he's in trouble, or his present boss is a yahoo.

2. If you're looking for salesmen with experience, make sure you find out in detail *what* experience they've had. Just seven years on the road is no use at all. Remember the old joke about the army good conduct medal—seven years of undetected crime. What you want to see are league standings, congratulatory memos from the boss, turnover graphs, commission statements, the salesman's own plan for how he covered his last territory, evidence of how he handled his reporting, his personal performance ratios and how these have steadily improved. He's also got to have a sound reason for wanting to leave his present company if he is successful. Beware of personality clashes with the boss—he may have one with you, too.

Any experienced salesman who cannot (or will not) produce such evidence has clearly not bothered collecting it, in which case he doesn't think right—and generally will be conning you into believing he's been successful when actually he's a failure.

3. Always, but *always*, check references. And don't ever do it by letter. Do it by telephone. No ex-boss is going to say anything nasty in writing about a past employee. But if you ask the right questions by telephone—open-ended questions (why, what, how, when, which, where, who)—you'll get the answers you're looking for.

4. Check even more thoroughly into work habits, motivation, how the prospective employee got on with his colleagues and superiors, if you are recruiting anyone *without* previous sales experience.

5. Before finally deciding, make up a foursome for dinner: you and your wife; he and his wife. Find out whether his wife is

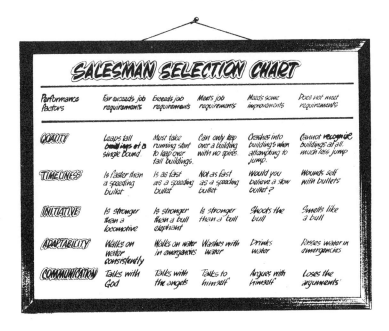

going to be an asset or a hindrance. If you've got two candidates who come pretty close, pick the one whose wife is going to back him up.

6. Beware of unmarried salesmen. Often they get even more tired than married ones, their territory plans frequently resemble that old joke about the sailor's wife in every port, and their shelter/security motivation levels can be quite low. But there are lots of exceptions.

And don't forget. . . .

When the new salesman starts work, give him a hero's welcome. Make him see that everyone thinks he is important. Get everyone properly briefed to make the new man's first few weeks as professional and as meaningful as they can be. Otherwise you'll probably de-motivate him before he even starts selling for you.

Remuneration Schemes

Most salesmen perform better if they have an incentive. So do most sales managers.

A person's basic salary should be high enough to satisfy his own and his family's basic needs: mortgage, food, clothes, school fees, furniture, vacations, eating out occasionally, and so on. If the salary doesn't achieve this, there could be problems with moonlighting, or worse. The salary should also be linked to the cost-of-living index—after all, the prices charged for the company's products or services are.

In addition to basic salary, the salesman and the manager should get some kind of commission on the total sales achieved.

Commission should *never* be paid on *all* sales achieved. Then it ceases to provide any incentive and becomes akin to the basic salary. Commission should start at a point on the sales turnover graph when the salesman's costs to the company have been covered—his breakeven point—or a little higher up the graph. Something like 75–80 percent of sales target is reasonable.

Then, the rate of commission should *increase* progressively as sales turnover increases—say, 1 percent from 80 percent to target; 1½ percent from target to 125 percent; 2 percent from 125 percent to 150 percent and (if the company can afford to lose the margin) 5 percent for any sales over 150 percent of target.

Targets, of course, have to be set properly, with the full involvement of the salesman, and be attainable. Read the sections on Forecasting and Setting Targets to find out how to achieve this.

Once properly set, targets should, like territories, be fixed, not adjusted annually. Thus, the salesman can see his efforts earning him more and more money, and the company makes more and more money likewise. Only if the product range is changed should targets be interfered with once they have been set and proved workable, too.

Read the section, "Growth," if this concept makes you uneasy.

Profitability bonuses are a waste of time. Every salesman knows that the directors, the accountants, and the auditors between them can make a laughing stock of the true profit situation—for good "tax avoidance" reasons, of course. If you want to add to the salary plus commission package, try some regular prize incentives, like vacations, color TVs, etc.

PAYING COMMISSION

To be really meaningful, commission should be calculated and paid on a monthly basis, not on an annual basis. This means that most companies will need to break their annual sales targets down into 12 individual monthly targets, allowing variations for seasonal demands if these apply.

The only snag with this system of monthly payments is that if the salesman has a few really good months in the first half of the year, and then his performance falls off during the second half, the company could wind up paying him too much commission. If the company takes the money back, by deducting it from the salesman's basic salary, this is bound to cause ill will. Thus, it is usual for only two thirds of due commission to be paid on a monthly basis, the balance being accumulated to form a lump sum at the end of the year, and from which any overpayments can be deducted. This also provides for the company which pays commission when the orders are actually received being able to deduct commission paid on any orders that are subsequently canceled.

Figure 22 shows a sample monthly commission statement. It caters to three product groups—two having the same commission rates but different "breakeven" or base points and targets, the third for, say, consumable items. There are many companies selling to industry where this type of format will fit, the main products being capital plant and the rest being materials, tooling, and consumables, for use with the capital plant.

WHAT ABOUT THE SALES MANAGER?

At the beginning of this section, I said that the manager as well as the salesman should be paid commission. I am amazed at the number of companies that expect their sales managers to lead the team well when their basic salaries are a couple of thousand dollars less than quite a few of their own salesmen's salary plus commission.

The manager's salary should be significantly more than the salesmen's salaries. His commission element should be in the form of an overriding commission, again with a rate increasing as sales turnover increases. He may also be penalized for any of his salesmen who do not perform for a predetermined period of time (no longer than three months, except for *new* salesmen).

Top executives should be paid this way, too. Then they'd stop moaning about paying their sales force far more than they are worth.

Name .... Area .... Period .... to ....

Objectives per Period	Group 1 Products	Group 2 Products	Groups 1 & 2 Total	Group 3 Products	Total
(1) Base					
(2) Target					
Cum. to Date					
(3) Base					
(4) Target					
Actual Sales Invoiced					
(5) For period					
(6) Cum. to date					

Commission Earned – Cumulative to Date

(7) First $ _____   (Max. line 4 minus 3)   at 1% $ _____
(8) Next $ _____   (Max. line 6 minus 4)   at 2% $ _____

(9) Total Sales $ _____   To agree with line 6

(10) Less: Already paid   – _____

(11) Now due (if negative treat as nil)
(12) Add: Group 3 commission at ½% Line 5
(13) Other commissions   _____

(14) Total Gross Commission
       Payable on Period – Payroll $ _____

(15) Advance herewith at ⅔ gross $ _____

Figure 22.   Monthly sales commission statement.

Sales Literature

I've tended to softpeddle the subject of training in this book, although training is a most important and ongoing requirement in any sales force.

My main reason for softpeddling is because I believe a good sales manager (with a little help from his friends) can cover most of his ongoing training requirements through the use of car cassette programs (see "Utilizing Traveling Time") and through the company's sales literature.

Just like the car cassette concept and my thoughts on trade cycles, I have found very few companies willing to adopt the concept of training through the sales literature. But I shall keep trying.

Consider the fundamentals: you train because you want the salesmen to do the job in a certain way, and to think in a certain way.

The salesmen, being human, seek to do the job in the easiest way they can find. Most of their thinking is linked to this easiest way.

The easiest way for a salesman to conduct a sales presentation is to use his sales literature as the main framework of the presentation. He therefore uses the literature, the words in the literature, the pictures in the literature, and the facts and figures in the literature.

The only snag is that the literature he uses wasn't designed to be his script for a sales presentation. It hardly ever contains anything about "what's in it for the customer." It rarely asks any questions. And it is never put together in the right order.

So most sales presentations which base themselves on the sales literature are something of a disaster.

Now, wouldn't it be much more logical to design the sales literature to say what you want the salesman to say when he conducts his presentation? All it means is that you translate your sales training program into words, pictures, and pages in brochures.

Then you have a "bible" which most of your salesmen will use automatically. In three months, they will know by heart the BEST METHOD OF PRESENTING THE PRODUCTS. And you didn't spend a penny of your training budget—it all came out of the sales promotion budget. Examples of "bible" literature, however, are very rare.

Service Contracts

Everyone in selling—the salesman, the area manager, the sales manager, the sales director—should have a written service contract. It should be not just the bare minimum to satisfy the statutory requirements, but a meaningful document which clearly defines what is what.

A properly designed service contract can do a lot to alleviate worry—that cancer which eats away at a person's performance in times when the going gets rough, when business is hard to get, when personalities clash. And you know it, there are plenty of those times.

A good service contract protects both the employee and employer, and it should. Here is a sample contract, with appropriate notes, which could be tailored to fit practically everyone in the sales team, from salesman to director.

Opening Paragraph

This agreement is made the ...... day of ......, 19....., between .... (hereinafter called the Company) of the one part and .... of .... (hereinafter called the Employee) of the other part.

Whereby It Is Agreed as Follows

The Company hereby engages the services of the Employee and the Employee accepts the employment by the Company as .... upon the terms and conditions hereinafter contained.

The employment shall begin on ...... and shall continue until determined in accordance with the provisions hereinafter contained.

Duties

The Employee shall under the direction of the Board of Directors of the Company (hereinafter called the Board) be responsible for and shall perform such duties and exercise such powers as from time to time may be assigned to or vested in him in such capacity by the Board.

(Note that authority comes from the Board, although the Employee may report to a manager who is not a member of the Board. Doing this enables the original contract to stay in force without major revision if the Employee is subsequently promoted from salesman to sales manager, or further. The details which do change are normally included in separate "Conditions of Employment" and "Job Description," which are referred to in the main Service Contract.)

Attention to Duties

The Employee, unless prevented by ill health, shall during the term of his employment devote the whole of his attention to the business of the Company. The Employee shall not, without the prior consent in writing of the Board, be directly or indirectly concerned in any other business during the term hereof.

(A "moonlighting" sales representative is a tired, de-motivated sales representative, setting a bad example to the rest of the team. Don't allow moonlighting of any kind, but be careful: the law requires in many cases that the "hours of business" be defined, outside of which you have no right to restrict an Employee. Check this with the Company's attornies.)

Remuneration

The Company shall pay to the Employee a salary of ..... per annum and such commission as the Conditions of Employment define. Such salary is to be paid in equal monthly installments in arrears on the last day of each month and such commission is to be paid as defined in the Conditions of Employment.

The said salary shall not be less than .... per annum and shall be reviewed on January 1 ...... and on January 1 in each succeeding year in accordance with the changes in the cost of living as indicated by the Consumer Price Index.

On January 1 .... and on January 1 of each succeeding year of the period of this agreement, the said sum of .... shall be increased by the percentage thereof, which corresponds to the percentage increase (if any) over the basic figure of the Index figure last published before the said review takes place.

(Note that the inclusion of such a cost-of-living clause may be deemed unenforceable if written during a time when it contravenes current government legislation. However, it does declare the company's intention, and, as such, is very reassuring to the Employee.)

Expenses

The Company shall reimburse to the Employee all reasonable traveling, hotel, and other expenses properly incurred in the performance of the Employee's duties hereunder.

Provision of Company Car

The Company shall provide the Employee with an automobile for the Employee's use, and shall pay all expenses of maintaining, servicing, and renewing the said automobile, including insurance and registration thereof, and shall reimburse the Employee the cost of all gasoline and oil consumed while said automobile is used for business purposes during the course of the employment of the Employee, as is stated hereunder.

(Note that it says nothing about private use, nor does it exclude private use. Thus, the Company can make a separate ruling on this if it wishes.)

Confidentiality

The Employee shall not (except in the proper course of his duties as described hereinunder) either during or after the period of his employment divulge to any person, and shall use the Employee's best endeavors to prevent the publication or disclosure of, any trade secret or manufacturing process or any information concerning the business or finances of the Company or any of its dealings, transactions, or affairs which have come to the Employee's knowledge during the course of his employment.

Company Property

Any equipment, papers, documents, sales aids, samples, records, and other articles supplied by the Company to the Employee remain the property of the Company and must not be damaged or destroyed by the Employee and on request by the Company or, if no longer required by the Employee, must be returned to the Company.

(Note that copies of any documents will be deemed by the courts to be the property of the owner of the original documents.)

Restraint Clauses

The Employee will not within the States of . . . .
(or wherever applicable) and within two years after ceasing to

be employed as hereinunder, without the previous consent of
the Board in writing, either alone or jointly with, or as manager or agent for, any person, firm, or company directly or
indirectly carry on or be engaged in the business of manufacturers and/or suppliers of ....
....
.... (list Company's products).
The Employee will not within two years of ceasing to be
employed as hereinunder, either on the Employee's own behalf or on behalf of any person, firm, or company, directly or
indirectly solicit, interfere with, or endeavor to entice away
from the Company any employee or any person, firm, or company who has at any time in the two years immediately preced-
ing the determination of the employment of the Employee
done business with the Company, provided that nothing contained in this clause shall be deemed to prohibit the Employee
seeking or procuring orders or doing business with persons,
firms, or companies in connection with businesses not related
or similar to the business of the Company.

Inventions

The Employee agrees that any invention, discovery, design,
or improvement made by the Employee at any time during
employment with the Company and in any way connected
with or applicable to the products manufactured by and sold
by—or the methods of manufacture of such products by—the
Company belongs to the Company, and that the Employee
will forthwith disclose the same to the Company and that:

1. The Employee will not without the written consent of the
Board apply for patents in any part of the world for any invention, discovery, design, or improvement so made by him.

2. The Employee will, if and whenever required to do so by
the Company, apply as nominee of the Company or join with
it in applying for patents in any part of the world for any
invention, discovery, design, or improvement so made by the

Employee as the Company shall in its sole discretion decide, and will at all times sign all such documents, and do all such things as may be requisite and desirable to vest the said patents when granted and all the right title and interest to and in the same in the Company absolutely as sole beneficial owner or as the Company may direct.

The Company agrees to pay all expenses in connection with such applications for patents by the Employee as nominee for or jointly with the Company, and will hold the Employee indemnified against all liabilities in connection with or arising out of such application or patents when granted.

The term "patents" in this agreement shall mean and include patents, brevet d'invention, petty patent, gebrauchmuster, utility model design registration, or any other form of protection or improvement that can be obtained in any part of the world.

(Note that every single employee of a company, from shop floor to directors, should agree to those "invention" clauses. The Company's life blood is at stake. I've seen far too many companies go bust because immoral employees have taken the best of the ideas, started up in competition, and stolen the market.)

Vacations

The Employee shall be entitled to such vacations with full pay as the Company shall notify the Employee are appropriate for the time being in accordance with the regulations of the Company relating thereto announced from time to time to the staff of the Company.

(Details are contained in the Employee's Conditions of Employment or a more general staff notice.)

Illness

The Company shall pay the aforementioned salary in full while the Employee shall be unable to fulfill the duties as hereinunder because of illness, physical or mental disability, or other cause beyond the employee's control up to a maximum period in the aggregate of 40 working days in any consecutive 52-week period. During any additional period of incapacity as aforesaid up to an additional period of 40 working days in any consecutive 52-week period, such salary shall be reduced by one half, and thereafter, until the Employee shall have resumed full duties, the Employee shall not be entitled to any salary.

(Note that often, companies add a clause covering a reduction of salary in proportion to payments received by employees while out sick; otherwise, some employees could earn more in their first 40 days while sick than while working.)

Pension Plan

The Employee, after completing the appropriate qualifying period, shall join the Company Contributory Pension Plan. The contribution level shall be that appropriate to the Employee's grade at the time of joining.

Termination of Employment

Except as hereinunder provided, this agreement shall continue in force unless determined during the first six months by either party giving the other one full calendar month's notice and thereafter three full calendar months' notice in writing. The company shall be entitled to give payment in lieu of notice.

If the Employee is at any time guilty of gross misconduct, neglect of duties, or refusal to carry out any order lawfully given to the Employee by the Company, then the Company shall be entitled to determine this agreement without notice or payment in lieu of notice.

The Company shall be entitled to terminate this agreement by notice in writing if the Employee shall be convicted of an indictable offense other than a traffic violation, provided that if the Employee shall have lost his driver's license as a result of a conviction for a traffic offense and in the opinion of the Board is unable to carry out the Employee's duties as hereinunder to the satisfaction of the Board, then the Company may terminate the employment of the Employee in the manner provided in this clause.

Dress

The Employee shall during the continuance of this agreement observe the requirements of the Company as to the style of dress and general appearance expected of a representative of the Company. Failure to so comply shall be grounds for determination as aforesaid.

Conclusion

As witness the hand of .... on behalf of .... and the hand of the Employee the day and year first above written
Signed by
On behalf of ....
In the presence of ....
Signed by ....
In the presence of ....
(Note that two copies of the agreement should be signed, both in the presence of witnesses—one copy for the Company, one for the Employee.) P.S. But don't put it all together yourself. Get the Company's attorney to do the final draft.

CONDITIONS OF EMPLOYMENT

Whether there is a properly drafted service agreement or not, every employer should give every employee the following information in writing. Items already covered in a service agreement may be omitted; the rest forming the "Conditions of Employment" document have already been referred to.

1. Name and address of employer and employee.
2. Date employment commences. (If previous service with another employer is regarded as part of the employment, as in a takeover situation or a transfer within a group, the *earliest* date of commencement is applicable.)
3. Salary level and methods of calculating all types of relevant remuneration.
4. Intervals at which payments are made.
5. Hours of work and any terms and conditions that apply.
6. Vacation benefits.
7. Terms and conditions relating to sickness or injury, including payment provisions.
8. Pension scheme details, including details of "contracting out" certificate if relevant.
9. Notice of termination periods.
10. Job title.
11. Specific disciplinary rules, other than those relating to health and safety.
12. Name of person to whom the employee should apply if he is dissatisfied with any disciplinary action taken against him.
13. Name and position of person to whom the employee can apply if seeking redress for any grievance relating to his employment.

Strengths and Weaknesses

You need to know your own, your company's, your competitors', your salesmen's, your market's, and your management team's. Make a list of all of them, a kind of "pro" and "con" list. And don't ever kid yourself.

Use the lists as the basis for your strategic and tactical planning, your training programs, your sales promotion plans, and for product development.

Supplier Evaluation

Is your company prepared and willing to submit itself to a Supplier Evaluation and Assessment? Have any of your present customers ever conducted one on you, or suggested the idea? As you expand your markets in the future, will you be ready for it when it happens?

Supplier Evaluation is a purchasing technique being introduced by more and more buying departments of large organizations. What the customers are trying to establish, in quantifiable terms, is their supplier's total capability to supply their requirements at the right time, in the right quality, and at the right price.

The forward-looking sales manager can prepare his company and his salesmen to meet the requirements of any such Evaluation or Assessment. This preparation usually takes the form of a specially designed piece of sales literature called a Company Profile. Build such a Profile into your budget, and you will not only put your company at the top of the league standings in the professional buyer's estimation; you will provide your salesmen with most of the ammunition and knowledge they need to master the commercial and financial aspects of their selling tasks.

A good Company Profile contains details of the company's capacity, plant and production equipment, inspection and test facilities, range of customers, future plans, ownership, key executives, and labor and financial record over the past five years.

Here are some of the questions to which a potential customer may require answers when conducting a Supplier Evaluation.

TECHNICAL ASPECTS

1. Has the supplier an adequate design staff?
2. Has the supplier effective quality control?
3. Is the technical staff sufficient to handle the volume of work we require plus the supplier's other commitments?

4. Are the test and inspection facilities and equipment adequate to meet our standards?
5. Are the facilities for handling rejects and repairs satisfactory?
6. Is the production plant and machinery good enough, reliable enough, and accurate enough to meet our standards?
7. Is there sufficient skilled manpower?
8. Is there adequate technical representation and liaison should the need arise?
9. Is the instruction and training facility adequate?
10. Is the supplier capable of interpreting our drawings and specifications?

COMMERCIAL ASPECTS

1. Are the supplier's financial resources adequate?
2. Is the management structure effective?
3. What is the supplier's delivery record?
4. How reliable and stable are the prices?
5. What are the supplier's relations with its own workforce like? Is the supplier "strike-prone"?
6. Has the supplier room for expansion if the need arose?
7. Is there adequate labor in the area?
8. Are the supplier's executives and customer-liaison people easy to communicate with?
9. Is the supplier easy to reach from our headquarters?
10. Has the supplier a reliable and professional purchasing-and-supply department and system within itself?
11. Does the supplier carry adequate stocks?
12. Is the guarantee satisfactory?
13. Has the supplier a competent accounts system that will deal quickly and simply with any invoice or account query?

14. Is the supplier's policy and procedure for rejects and returns satisfactory?
15. Has the supplier adequate transport?
16. Is the sales force competent and available quickly?

QUESTIONS FOR OVERSEAS AGENTS AND IMPORTERS

1. Has the agent adequate technical knowledge of his principal's products?
2. Can the agent give the necessary technical back-up and advice?
3. Is the agent competent with his import procedures?
4. What are his relations with his principals?
5. Is he financially sound?

THIRD-PARTY REFERENCE

After you have answered all these questions, the potential customer is more than likely going to finish up by asking you for the names of at least three of your regular established customers that he can contact and find out what they *really* think of you as a supplier. So have some good "third-party references" already primed and available.

TRAITOR

I spend a fair proportion of my consultancy time sorting out purchasing departments as well as sales departments. Let's face it; shouldn't supply and demand be as close together as possible?

Here is a list of questions I suggest that buyers should ask the many, many salesmen who persist in wasting their time rather than getting down to business. You may care to pass this list on

to your own salesmen and tell them to be sure they have the
answers for every call they make.

1. Why did you take the trouble to come and see me?
2. Why do you feel your products will be of benefit to us?
3. Why do you feel your product is better for us than the
   one we are using?
4. What will we gain by using or selling this?
5. Please, your time as well as my time is very expensive.
   Can you get to the point?

Team Spirit

Don't ever let your salesmen feel that they are in competition
with one another. If they do, they'll hold back vital information which could be of benefit to everyone.

Every time you get the sales force together, devote at least
half an hour to a brainstorming session. Get the team working
as a team. Pick one thorny general objection for each meeting,
and get everyone contributing to find the best way of dealing
with that objection. Then make sure each and every one of
your salesmen can *use* that best way. Do this consistently for a
few months and everyone will get the message.

It's teamwork that gets the best results.

Territories and Targets

Once you have got them right, don't ever change the salesmen's territories. This will de-motivate, as nothing else will.

Only if a salesman leaves can you afford to review the territory situation, and then only very carefully.

Likewise, if you have set targets linked to commission earnings, those targets, once set, should remain the same. That is

not to say that your *sales turnover* targets should be frozen; only the *base* targets from which commission payments begin.

In other words, if a salesman develops his territory over a number of years, he should be rewarded progressively for all his efforts in this development, not chopped back each year and be made to start all over again for the same amount of commission earnings. Don't be greedy, or you will lose your best men.

Only in the event of price increases should commission-related base targets be amended. Everyone will see this as fair. It's really the number of orders that count.

THESE SALESMEN FAILED TO MAKE TARGET

Titles

Don't use titles indiscriminately. Don't make a salesman an area manager unless he's got at least one salesman to manage. Don't ever use titles to motivate a salesman. You'll upset your company's management structure, and you'll have a hard time getting it right again.

Have a sliding scale of sizes of company car and use this instead. You'll find it much more effective and it gives you only *one* problem—overcoming the internal politics of giving a senior salesman a bigger car than the one belonging to the Vice-President, Finance. Don't laugh; this is true for most of the world's business.

Trade Cycles

Don't let them fool you. Don't even believe them.

I've lost count of the number of times I've helped a company's products take off like a rocket when all their competitors in the market were going downhill fast in accordance with the known trade cycle.

For example, we introduced a brand new machine—a Russian machine—in the British market at a time when the trade cycle for home market machine tool sales was declining at 30 percent to the vertical. A new approach to the techniques of selling machine tools, based on finance, not on product features; a one-day training course on how to demonstrate the new machines; a press conference and press demonstration; and some different advertising over a three-month period helped the importing company increase its home market share from 2 percent to 50 percent in one year. Total cost of devising the marketing plan, training the sales force, designing the literature and advertisements, and handling press relations— $15,000.

All it needed was a bit of original salesmanship and some enthusiasm. Everyone else was just sitting back and kidding themselves that there was no point trying to sell that year, because the trade cycle said it wasn't possible.

If you *really* want an excellent example of how a whole industry has kidded itself for more than 20 years, it has to be the British machine tool industry. All the major manufacturers in this industry advocate limiting major machine tool trade exhibitions in Britain to once every four years. They say they cannot afford more frequent exhibitions.

"So what have exhibitions got to do with trade cycles and people kidding themselves?" you may be saying. Well, consider the graph in Figure 23. It depicts net home market machine tool orders since 1957, adjusted to take out all price increases. Pinpointed on this graph, you see the times Britain held its major International Machine Tool Shows. Do you think it's coincidence that the date of the show always coincides with a peak in the trade cycle?

No. The peaks in this particular trade cycle have to be caused by the International Machine Tool Shows themselves. Consider how all the salesmen in the machine tool industry would react to the news that in six months' time, they will again spend ten days whooping it up at the big exhibition. Consider all the new sales literature, new models, additional advertising, press releases, invitations to customers, etc., going out during the six-month build-up to each show. Consider how all this activity would bolster the enthusiasm of practically every salesman in the machine tool business—and how easy it would be to convert some of this enthusiasm into extra business.

And in the six months after each show, consider how long it would take these same salesmen to follow up all the inquiries they generated during the shows themselves, and how many of these inquiries they would convert into orders.

It's just a whole industry jumping up and down at the same time—extra activity and enthusiasm equals a rising trade cycle.

If you really want to wonder what's going on in this country,

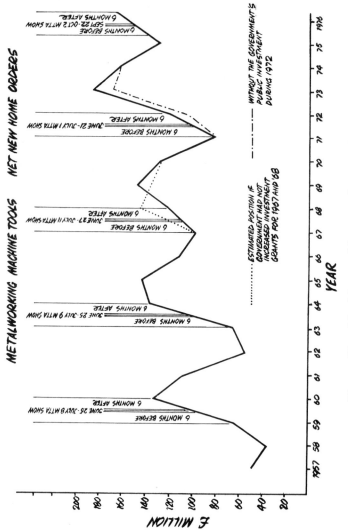

Figure 23.   Machine tool home orders graph.

match my graph with the national trade cycle for Britain and with the trade cycle for Western Europe. Then tell me it's just a coincidence that they all look so much alike!

Machine tools is one of Britain's general economic indicators. The trend is set by machine tools; everything else tends to follow. So ask yourself why the machine tool industry is still advocating exhibitions every four years, when it could change Britain's trade cycle from, say, a four-year loop to a two-year loop, simply by having its major show every two years?

(The American machine tool industry woke up to this in the mid-1960s. Since then, the Chicago show has been held every two years. Their British counterparts have recently seen the light—a mere 15 years later—and the two-year cycle began in 1980.)

Okay, if you believe only half of all that, what are you going to do to thumb your nose at your own trade cycle? Because if it's true for machine tools, its true for every other industry.

All you've got to do is sell it to them!

Training Salesmen

Training is the key factor of personal development, and without personal development your salesmen will quickly get fed up and leave for greener pastures.

The development of a salesman need not necessarily be aimed at promotion to management. Many managers never realize this. A salesman can be developed so that he remains happy being a salesman, yet his abilities and his knowledge should be regularly updated so that his value to the company is continually increasing, and he can see that this is so.

There are at least eight different areas of the selling job where regular and continuous training is essential:

1. Product knowledge.
2. Application knowledge.

3. Competitors' products and applications.
4. Customers' businesses and their trends.
5. Customers' markets and their trends.
6. Selling techniques.
7. Planning techniques.
8. Commercial and financial knowledge.

If you do some of this training yourself, make sure your presentation is as professional as if you were negotiating the biggest order of your life. Prepare everything, lay out the meeting room properly, ban all interruptions, use professionally produced visual aids, provide refreshments, and above all, get the objectives clear, and make the whole proceedings look to everyone there as if they are critically important—which they are.

Unwinding

How do you unwind after a hard day at the office, or out in the field?

Stereo? Scotch? Squash? Sex?

You need something. I've got a Ludwig drum set permanently set up in my den, with 80 watts of quadraphonic to back it up. Ten minutes beating the hell out of that to Count Basie and I'm a new man.

People who cannot unwind get very tired very fast. Find a way that fits you, and find it fast.

U.S.P.

Whatever happened to U.S.P.?

In the days before marketing clouded everyone's thoughts on what selling and sales management were all about, U.S.P. was a critical part of the manager's training armory.

It stands for Unique Selling Point.

Every product has at least one; otherwise, no one would ever buy the product. U.S.P. is the "edge" your product has over its competitors. U.S.P. is the "difference" which makes customers buy yours rather than someone else's or something else.

Find out what the U.S.P. is for every one of your products or services. And once you know, don't lose sight of the fact that if you are up against strong competition, U.S.P. is all you've got to sell.

Utilizing Traveling Time

I've got a hobby horse.

I've had it for at least five years. It frustrates me, it infuriates me. I cannot understand why someone, somewhere doesn't do something about it. I've tried many times to interest sales managers and directors in the concept, but I've never once succeeded. So maybe it's a lousy concept. I don't think so, and I'll never have a better opportunity of shouting about it, so here goes. . . .

More than 40 percent of a salesman's total time is spent in his car, traveling from A to B and back again. Apart from a little thinking from time to time about what happened on the last call, and what is likely to happen on the next, this 40 percent of total time is pretty useless for the salesman—and for his company.

So how about using it for ongoing PRODUCT TRAINING and APPLICATION TRAINING and for disseminating information about the competition, the markets, changes in company policies, *and* for those frequent inspirational messages from the boss?

All you need to do is equip each salesman's car with a cassette player and provide him, through the mail, with the necessary cassette tapes. Ten minutes maximum of business on each tape, laced with some good music, and finishing with some key questions each salesman has to answer, just to make sure he plays the tape.

The initial investment on equipment would be amortized against just one day's meeting at headquarters of the whole sales force.

Producing the tapes is easy. You could do it at home or get a couple of members of the local operatic society to do the voices. Writing a script is no more difficult than preparing a proposal or a new piece of sales literature.

SELLING TECHNIQUES

And if the concept works for you on product training, why not try it on salesmanship? How's this for a list of ten-minute cassettes—cassettes which the salesman can select and play while he is on his way to an important call?

Tape 1: What's the objective of your next call? How can you best start the interview?

Tape 2: You're going to conduct a detailed survey. What do you need, what do you look for, what questions do you need to ask the prospect?

Tape 3: You're taking a prospect to a demonstration. What does the prospect really need to see, what could go wrong, and why?

Tape 4: You're following up the quotation. How do you get him to say yes? What objections might you have to deal with? Do you know the best answers?

Tape 5: How can you persuade the prospect to give us a chance? He's been dealing with our competitors for so long, how best can you find out his criteria for ordering and match it to our products?

Tape 6: Is your offer cost-effective? Have you taken the trouble to find out how much the customer is going to make, or save, if he buys our product? And have you told him in a way that will enable him to convince his own directors?

Tape 7: What's in it for the customer? You know all the main features of our products—how the customer benefits from these features—but do you tell him?

Tape 8: Prospecting. Which companies are most likely to buy our products—and why? Just exactly what are we selling—what is our "edge"?

Tape 9: Getting more appointments, and at the best times. Dealing with the inquiries generated by our advertising.

Tape 10: Territory planning. What are you doing sitting in that car for 40 percent of the day, when with a little attention to the routes you take, you could spend at least 10 percent of the wasted time selling to someone else?

And for the way home:

Tape 11: You lost the order. Why? Can you make sure you never make the same mistake again?

Just as a bonus, here are a couple of tapes for the sales manager who, of course, needs to be fully conversant with all 11 of them.

Tape 12: Training salesmen on the job. What to do with that one day a month out there in the field with each man?

Tape 13: Counseling. You have a salesman with a problem. What do you do about it—and how?

That's my hobby horse, then. Any takers?

Figure 24.   GKN–Sankey supermatic demo panel.

Visual Aids

Give your salesmen some kind of effective visual aids which they can use to back up their verbal presentations, preferably something the customers can get their hands on. The literature is never enough.

If you are selling fasteners, make sure all your salesmen carry, and use, the widest selection of samples. Likewise, if you are selling castings, cut away to show the texture and uniformity of grain if this is important.

If you sell switchgear, electronic components, instrumentation controls, anything small and intricate, make sure your salesmen have plenty of bits and pieces for the customers to play with.

Samples of this kind are critical.

The largest vending-machine company in Great Britain, GKN–Sankey, introduced a new model in 1977 with a unique digital drink selection panel, like a giant pocket calculator. Each salesman was provided with a panel, straight out of production, which he could use to demonstrate to a customer how the new digital system worked (Figure 24). The customers and the salesmen were delighted—both with the sample panel, complete with special carrying case, and with how easy it made explaining and understanding the new machine.

Why Not, Why Not?

I've pinched this from Sir Barnes Wallis, the aircraft designer responsible for those fantastic bouncing bombs used by the Dam Busters in World War II, blockbuster "earthquake" bombs, and a host of other way out but highly successful devices. It's his favorite expression.

Sir Barnes Wallis never conformed to traditional ways of doing a job. He looked for, and found, the different approach. A good sales manager should think this way—always on the lookout for a better way of selling or presenting a product, or designing an advertisement, or packaging or exhibiting. It is the *gimmick* that whets the appetite of the customer these days. As long as it is a good gimmick. So forget about the conventions and the traditional ways of doing the job. Be original, and be more successful.

Xmas Presents

The only kind of Christmas present worth giving a customer is one that will stay in his place of business for a long time (at least until *next Christmas*), reminding him every day that you are one of his most reliable and loyal suppliers.

Cases of whiskey, once drunk, are soon forgotten. Presents that the customer takes home to his wife are likewise out of sight and out of mind.

So don't ever lose sight of the fact that Christmas presents are part of your *sales promotion* budget. Give presents that *are* strictly sales promotion and you maximize the return on the investment, as well as avoiding all hints of bribery and corruption.

The list of things you can give customers at Christmas time is endless. Prices, too, can range from a few dollars to a few hundred. Whatever you choose, always make sure your company name, address, and telephone number is on the gift, and always bear in mind that the gift *must* reflect the corporate identity of your company.

What I mean by that is if you sell cheap and cheerful products, you can bestow a cheap and cheerful gift. If you sell the best and most expensive products, your gifts need to match this.

THE ULTIMATE GIFT

The perfect business gift, the ultimate, used to sit on my office desk, black and slightly sinister, bearing the name, address, and telephone number of the firm that gave it to me (Figure 25).

A slot in its top took a quarter. The coin rested in the slot, making an electrical contact which caused the whole box to vibrate, heave about, and emit a gravelly, graveyard-style, grinding noise. A trap door in the top then slowly opened, a horrible green slimy hand crept out and gently took hold of the quarter. And then—faster than the eye could follow—hand and coin were gone, trap door was closed tight, and the black box was still and silent.

You had to see it to appreciate the artistry of the mechanism.

So consider the factors that make this black box the ultimate business gift. It sits on a customer's desk, making him money. Every time someone tries it, he makes 25¢. Your competitor visits him, sees your name on the box, and says, "What's this?"

The customer smiles and replies, "It'll cost you a quarter to find out." (Have you ever taken money from the competition before?)

If the box goes wrong, the customer loses his income from it and the pleasure he gets from showing people the thing. So he telephones you.

Certainly you can replace it. "Oh, by the way, what is happening with that job we discussed last month?" you can ask.

Figure 25.   Black box—the ultimate business gift.

Yahoo

If you don't know what it means, look it up in a dictionary.

You will be well on the way to being one, when your staff starts hanging notices like this all around the office:

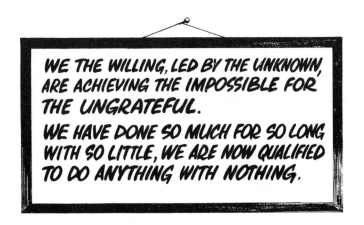

WE THE WILLING, LED BY THE UNKNOWN, ARE ACHIEVING THE IMPOSSIBLE FOR THE UNGRATEFUL.
WE HAVE DONE SO MUCH FOR SO LONG WITH SO LITTLE, WE ARE NOW QUALIFIED TO DO ANYTHING WITH NOTHING.

Zest

Don't ever let the zest go out of the job. Don't let the brass get you down, or the job start running you. If you do, you might as well give up and start growing mushrooms.

Always let your salesmen see your best side. Keep that lousy feeling for when you get home. I know it's not fair on the wife, but she'll understand; your salesmen won't.

Your job satisfaction is just as important as your salesmen's. I hope this book will help you put a little more zest into your job and provide you with a few tips that will help you increase your job satisfaction, your results, and your take-home pay.

Postscript

THE INDISPENSABLE MAN

Sometimes, when you're feeling important
Sometimes, when your Ego's in bloom,
Sometimes, when you take it for granted
You're the best informed man in the room,
Take a bucket, and fill it with water;
Put your hand in it, up to the wrist;
Pull it out, and the hole that remains there
Is the measure of how you'll be missed.
You may splash all you please as you enter.
You may stir up the water galore.
But stop! and you'll see in a moment
That it looks just the same as before.
The moral of this simple story
Is, do just the best that you can,
Because you'll find that in spite of vainglory,
There is no "Indispensable Man."

Source unknown

MEMO REF:

THE CURRENT CRISIS

In view of the current financial crisis the following figures may be of interest:

Population of Country	220,000,000
People aged 65 and over	60,000,000
Balance left to do the work	160,000,000
People aged 18 and under	80,000,000
Balance left to do the work	80,000,000
Union members	40,000,000
Balance left to do the work	40,000,000
People in Armed Forces	10,000,000
Balance left to do the work	30,000,000
Government, local government and other civil servants	25,000,000
Balance left to do the work	5,000,000
People who won't work	4,700,000
Balance left to do the work	300,000
People in prison	299,998
Balance left to do the work	2

You and I, therefore, must work harder, particularly you, as I am really fed up with running this joint on my own.